CITYSPOTS
ISTANL

Sean Sheehan

Page 60 MAP
in la Blue Mosque.

Pag. 74 MAP
1-10 GRAND BAZAAR

Page 50 underground?

55 BOS
56 TRAIN TAXI

Written by Sean Sheehan
Original photography by Sean Sheehan
Front cover photography courtesy of Giovanni Simeone/4cornersimages.com
Series design based on an original concept by Studio 183 Limited

Produced by Cambridge Publishing Management Limited
Project Editor: Tim Ryder
Layout: Trevor Double
Maps: PC Graphics
Transport map: © Communicarta Ltd

Published by Thomas Cook Publishing
A division of Thomas Cook Tour Operations Limited
Company Registration No. 1450464 England
PO Box 227, Unit 18, Coningsby Road
Peterborough PE3 8SB, United Kingdom
email: books@thomascook.com
www.thomascookpublishing.com
+ 44 (0) 1733 416477

ISBN-13: 978-184157-633-6
ISBN-10: 1-84157-633-6

First edition © 2006 Thomas Cook Publishing
Text © 2006 Thomas Cook Publishing
Maps © 2006 Thomas Cook Publishing
Series Editor: Kelly Anne Pipes
Project Editor: Ross Hilton
Production/DTP: Steven Collins

Printed and bound in Spain by GraphyCems

CONTENTS

SYMBOLS & ABBREVIATIONS

The following symbols are used throughout this book:

ⓐ address ☎ telephone ⓕ fax ⓔ email ⓦ website address
🕐 opening times Ⓝ public transport connections ❶ important

The following symbols are used on the maps:

🛈	information office	○	city
✈	airport	○	large town
✚	hospital	○	small town
🛡	police station	═	motorway
🚌	bus station	▬	main road
🚆	railway station	▬	minor road
Ⓜ	metro	▬	railway
✝	cathedral		
❶	numbers denote featured cafés & restaurants		

Hotels and restaurants are graded by approximate price as follows:
£ budget **££** mid-range **£££** expensive

◗ *Enter Istanbul: worlds within worlds at the Blue Mosque*

INTRODUCING
Istanbul

Introduction

You probably have a nodding acquaintance with the clichés that
circulate about Istanbul; the clash of cultures, if not civilisations,
East meets West, and so on. Well, just leave them on the carousel at
Atatürk International Airport, for they have only a historical truth
and, like the new Turkish currency that has discarded six zeros in
one fell swoop, different values are now in play. Istanbul does
straddle the Bosphorus – the narrow stretch of sea that,
geographically, divides Europe from Asia – but the 12 million or more
who inhabit the split megalopolis are exercised not with supposed
geopolitical fault lines but with a perceived need for a modern
transport system connecting the city's different quarters. For the
visitor, though, the waters that break up the city – not once but
twice – are part of its charm. This is Venice on a colossal scale,
not so posh perhaps, but magnificently more blessed in its past
glories, and spiced up with an elegant hedonism that surprises
and delights.

Like any world city on the scale of Istanbul, there are
neighbourhoods and districts with distinct identities, but even on
a short visit you can dip into all of the most appealing. The old
city, Sultanahmet, evocative of the worlds of the Roman and
Ottoman empires, is the preferred destination for many travellers.
Most of the historical and cultural attractions are to be found
here, and at night, when Sultanahmet's skyline is lit up by ancient
mosques and their minarets, a special atmosphere prevails. Across
the Golden Horn, a narrow inlet of water that divides European
Istanbul, there are more narrow, cobbled streets with flavours of
the past, but also a more contemporary and cosmopolitan city.
Here you will find bars, pavement cafés, nightclubs, design-

focused restaurants, art galleries, food stalls and a swinging population of the young and young-at-heart.

Istanbul is a place to enjoy and remember where the past and the present mingle effortlessly. Most astonishing for a city of its size and diversity, the people are easy-going and friendly and the safety factor is remarkably high.

△ *Feeling peckish? Try some delicious local specialities from a street vendor*

When to go

CLIMATE

Between November and late March, the days and nights can be chilly with temperatures ranging between 2° and 10°C (35° and 50°F) and sunshine at a premium. Mid-April to the end of May and the autumn months of September and October are ideal in terms of mild weather and plenty of sunshine. From the end of May to August visitor numbers soar, temperatures range between 18° and 28°C (64° and 82°F) and there is a daily average of ten hours of sunshine.

SEASONAL ATTRACTIONS

Istanbul can be enjoyed at any time of the year and there are advantages to being there between November and late March when visitor numbers are at their lowest. The major sites and attractions are not plagued with coach parties, restaurants are less likely to be full and discounted rates are often available at hotels. Spring brings the opening of rooftop terraces for alfresco wining and dining, fresh fruits enhance breakfast buffets and dessert menus, and the city's green areas blossom with colourful flowers. The light and sound show at the Blue Mosque gets underway in May and lasts until September. The summer months and the long days of sunshine bring crowds to the city, the cultural calendar fills with events and an air of festivity characterises the bars and pavement cafés. The long days continue through autumn but the city is not so busy and there is still a lot happening on the cultural front.

ANNUAL EVENTS

The website of the Istanbul Foundation for Culture and Arts, www.iksv.org/english, is a good source of information for the cultural events listed here and more. Check out www.mymerhaba.com for insider information on current and cultural matters. The following are some of the main regular events held in and around the city.

April

The **International Istanbul Film Festival** kicks off in April in a number of venues, mainly in Beyoğlu. **Independence Day** on 23 April,

◐ *The Turkish sunshine beats down*

commemorating the establishment of the Turkish Republic in 1923, is marked by live music and a grand parade of children in folk costumes. This event takes place on İstiklal Caddesi in Beyoğlu and begins in the morning.

May–July
The **International Istanbul Theatre Festival** takes place in May–June and the main venue is the Atatürk Cultural Centre in Taksim Square (see page 104). The **International Istanbul Music and Dance Festival** usually takes place in mid-June and early July and two main venues are used, the Hagia Eirene Museum and the Atatürk Cultural Centre. Most of the theatrical events are in Turkish, but the music festival features performances of music from all around the world. The first week in July also sees the launch of the two-week-long **International Istanbul Jazz Festival** (www.iksv.org/caz/english).

August
Turkey's biggest open-air music festival, **Rock'n Coke** (www.pozitif-ist.com), is held every year at Hezarfen Airport, 50 km (30 miles) outside Istanbul by the shores of Lake Buyukcekmece. It attracts national and international music stars, plus an audience of around 40,000, and lasts three days.

September–October
The **Akbank Jazz Festival** (www.pozitif-ist.com) is not as big as the July jazz festival but there will still be many special performances in places like Babylon (see page 99) and the Nardis Jazz Club (see page 99).

September–November

The **International Istanbul Biennial** occurs every two years, scheduled next for 2007, and features exhibitions of paintings and other visual arts.

November

The **Efes Pilsen Blues Festival** takes place in November in a variety of venues around the city.

PUBLIC HOLIDAYS

Secular

New Year's Day 1 January	**Victory Day** 30 August
Independence Day 23 April	**Republic Day** 29 October
Youth and Sports Day 19 May	

Religious

The date of the Muslim holy month of **Ramazan** (Ramadan), governed by a lunar calendar, occurs 11 days earlier each year, beginning on 13 September in 2007 and on 2 September in 2008. Muslims refrain from eating and drinking between dawn and dusk, but most restaurants and bars remain open. While non-Muslim visitors are not inconvenienced, it is only polite not to make a show of eating or drinking during the day. The end of Ramazan is celebrated with the three-day **Şeker Bayramı** (Sugar Festival) and the festival is a national holiday, with banks and offices closed. **Kurban Bayramı** (Feast of the Sacrifice), commemorating Abraham's willingness to sacrifice his son, is celebrated two months later and lasts four days, with banks and many offices closed.

Catching the eye of the sultan

A Turkish warrior tribe called the Ottomans or Osmanlis, named after an early ruler, Osman I, conquered Constantinople in 1453 and as a consequence the Roman empire ceased to exist. It was a momentous event in world history and the Ottomans went on to rule an enormous area that took in the Middle East, North Africa and a swathe of Europe. The Ottoman empire, based in Istanbul, was ruled by Turkish emperors known as sultans, and Mehmet II, the sultan who conquered Constantinople, set about refashioning his new capital. He turned St Sophia, the great church built under a Christian emperor of Rome in the 6th century, into a mosque and ordered the building of a palatial residence and seat of government, Topkapı Palace. The most exclusive part of his new palace would be strictly off-limits to most males except for the sultan and his family, hence its name, harem, from an Arabic word meaning 'forbidden', and the sultan's brothers would be permanent guests in a special area called the Cage, thus avoiding nasty intrigues over succession.

The harem, with over 400 rooms for the sultan's wives, concubines and slaves, was guarded over by black eunuchs who were allowed to enter only during the day. Such was the secrecy surrounding the women of the harem that rumour was rife and stories spread about the ruler of the harem, always the mother of the ruling sultan, known as the valide sultan. Her authority was unquestioned and while the valide sultan enjoyed a life of luxury, the same was not true for the majority of the hundreds of female slaves under her control. Most of them were taken as captives from their homes in the Caucasus or from the west in Poland and Hungary and their only chance of a good life came if they caught the eye of the sultan. If promoted to the status of concubine, they had a relatively luxurious lifestyle and, if they bore a child, rose to dizzy new heights of indulgence and were given their own apartments; those who remained unnoticed by the sultan remained slaves and lived fairly desperate lives until they died.

⬤ *Constantinople's chains across the sea were no match for Ottoman armies*

History

The origins of Istanbul's significance lies with its location astride an ancient trade route between the Mediterranean and Asia. The Greeks founded city-states on both the European and Asian sides of the Bosphorus and one of these, Byzantium, was conquered by the Romans in 64 BC. In the 4th century AD the Roman emperor Constantine relocated his capital to Byzantium and the city became known as Constantinople. When barbarian hordes stormed the gates of Rome a century later, the Greek-speaking and Christianised Constantinople survived in the east. A thousand years later it was still ruled by emperors who called themselves Roman and the city became the mainstay of what became known as the Byzantine empire, enfolding the Mediterranean littoral from Spain to Syria. The Byzantine era is the context for some of the most monumental structures that visitors flock to see today, including Aya Sofya (see page 64), the church of St Sofia built under Emperor Justinian in the 6th century. Five centuries later, the empire was still pulling rank under not Buffy, but Basil the Bulgar-slayer, and a hundred years later, when western Europe had emerged from the dark ages, more people still lived in Constantinople than in Rome, London and Paris combined.

Empires come and go, however, and in 1453 it was the turn of the Ottomans to rule the roost and Topkapı Palace (see page 66) was built as the palatial pad for a reign of sultans with names like Süleyman the Magnificent, Selim the Sot and İbrahim the Mad. Notwithstanding the nomenclature, the Ottomans were remarkably resilient and survived for over four hundred years. It was not until the early 20th century that, finding itself on the losing side in World War I, the Ottoman empire saw itself at the mercy of the victors.

It was the end of Ottoman rule but, when Greek armies invaded Anatolia in 1919, a resurgent nationalism asserted itself and the Turkish War of Independence led to the creation of a Turkish Republic in 1923. The young soldier who emerged from the War of Independence as the saviour of the nation was Mustafa Kemal Paşa and he was proclaimed Atatürk ('Father of the Turks').

Democracy came to Turkey in the wake of World War II and, although there were military coups in 1960, 1971 and again in 1980, the country is now a stable constitutional state. A collapse of the Turkish economy in 2001 led to a new government and plans are well under way for the country to eventually join the EU. Although the issue is as hotly debated within Turkey as it is within some of the existing EU member states, it is not difficult to imagine the citizens of Istanbul embracing another change of identity – this, after all, is part of what their history has always been about.

ATATÜRK'S ACHIEVEMENTS

As well as being the founder, Atatürk was the first president of the Republic of Turkey. He carried out many reforms, such as replacing the Arabic alphabet with a Roman one and encouraging the population to adopt a Western style of dress. In an attempt to signal Turkey's new identity, Atatürk shifted the nation's capital from Istanbul to Ankara.

Lifestyle

Arriving by air in daylight, you will be afforded an aerial view of the vast size and spread of the city and when you do land and mingle with the crowds on the street, the rather special lifestyle of Istanbullas will gradually make itself felt. As with most cities with a population of 12 million (and some estimates make it closer to 15 million or more), Istanbul is a bustling and cosmopolitan metropolis where most people are busy going about the business of living. Yet what emerges as a pleasant surprise is an impression of people not harassed by urban pressures or borne down by the stress of work but, instead, rather well adjusted to a chosen pace of life that allows for relaxation. Cups of tea and coffee are not gulped down in between rushing off to that next deadline – though the cups are so inordinately small you could be forgiven for thinking they were designed for just that purpose – but sipped leisurely and made to last for extended bouts of convivial conversation. This is a city more happy with itself than one might expect, considering the hustle and bustle and the mix of ethnicities, and there is a strong sense of people living together on their own terms of civility and sociability.

Aspects of this very public lifestyle are there to be encountered on the street and even the hustlers in Sultanahmet who try to inveigle you into their carpet shops do so with charm and courtesy and if you appear cross at their antics they wonder why you are being so disagreeable. There is always time, it seems, to take a drink and have a chat and this is nowhere so apparent as in the pavement cafés and alfresco bars that litter the city when the winter cold has passed and the days are long and warm. The stupendous grandeur of three past civilizations and the minaret-studded cityscape is taken for granted by Istanbullas, who see it all as their glorious backdrop for romancing the city and making and sustaining friendships, as well as making a living and getting by.

⬥ *The blue eye brings luck, so is often hung outside of front doors*

Culture

History provides a clue to the astonishing richness and diversity of the city's culture and the Archaeological Museum (see page 63) opens a window on the ancient background and broader context that the city has shared in for so many centuries. The millennium-long Byzantine empire, when Istanbul was called Constantinople, a world capital and the richest city in Christendom, nurtured a flowering of the arts and created structures like the Aya Sofya (see page 64), the Hippodrome (see page 62), Valens Aqueduct (see page 79) and the Basilica Cistern (see page 62). It is the richness of this cultural legacy that makes Sultanahmet such an attractive base for accommodation in the city because this area was the heart of Constantinople and there are reminders of the Byzantine past everywhere you look and walk.

A new cultural chapter begins even before the final conquest of Constantinople in 1453 by the Ottomans when Rumeli Hisarı (see page 123) was built on the Bosphorus. In the city itself, Ottoman architecture expressed itself in the mighty Topkapı Palace (see page 66) and, as part of an empire founded on the Muslim faith, in the building of the many great mosques that continue to adorn the city. Chief among these cultural highlights are the Blue Mosque (see page 64) and the magnificent Süleymaniye Camii complex (see page 78). For many, however, Islamic art is at its finest not on the monumental scale but in the intricate detail of mosaics and calligraphy, and the best place to appreciate these art forms is in the Museum of Turkish and Islamic Arts (see page 66) and the Calligraphy Museum (see page 80). Ottoman culture also imbued

● *The Archaeological Museum gives an insight into Turkey's rich history*

European influences and these can be appreciated in the 19th-century décor of Dolmabahçe Palace (see page 106).

Istanbul is anything but a shrine to ancient cultural forms, however, and the contemporary arts scene finds expression in a number of new galleries that have opened in the last couple of years. Pride of place goes to the waterside Istanbul Modern (see page 92), a converted warehouse with large open spaces for exhibitions of paintings, sculptures and installation art. Close on its heels are two other galleries, the Pera Museum (see page 92) which is also in Beyoğlu and which is currently hosting an exhibition of Henri Cartier-Bresson's photographs, and the Sabancı Müzesi (see page 124), which is further afield and on the shores of the Bosphorus at Emirgan. The fact that it is currently hosting an exhibition of Picasso gives some idea of its privately funded clout and makes a journey there worthwhile.

MOSQUE CULTURE

Non-Muslim visitors are welcome at all Istanbul mosques and, like any place of worship, proprieties should be observed. Shoes are removed before entry and bare arms and legs should be covered. Men remove hats or caps and women cover their hair with a scarf. There are five daily prayer times, each lasting 30 or 40 minutes, during which time you should not wander around devotees. The main prayer session takes place on a Friday and visiting a mosque should be avoided on this day. There is no charge for visiting a mosque but, when leaving, it is courteous to make a contribution to the donation box.

● *The Blue Mosque – a gem in the heart of Istanbul*

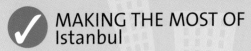

MAKING THE MOST OF
Istanbul

Shopping

Shopping is easy in Istanbul, offering variety and choices for all budgets and, while payment can be made with a credit card in most places, many shops will offer a small discount equivalent to the card company charge if you pay in cash. Bargaining is not practised in the brand-name or upmarket stores, nor is it generally expected where the price of items is clearly marked – especially with lower-priced souvenirs. However, when it comes to purchases in shops aimed at visitors, you can be fairly sure that some haggling is expected. When battling for a bargain, keep it courteous at all times and try to have some idea of what the merchandise is worth (or at least what it is worth to you). Try not to be the first to make an offer and when you do, ensure it is less than what you are prepared to pay.

WHERE TO SHOP

The Grand Bazaar (see page 76) is the most renowned shopping area for carpets, jewellery, leather jackets, handicrafts and souvenirs and you have some 4,000 shops to choose from. Bargains, though, are rare and haggling is an art form that the vendors have more skill at than most punters. The Spice Bazaar (see page 78) is smaller and can be more satisfying. For general merchandise and fashion in all its guises, pedestrianised İstiklal Caddesi is the place to start, though there are a number of interesting little shops tucked away off it in the back streets of Galatasaray. Here you will also find antiquities of an affordable kind as well as one-off items of clothing. For souvenirs, schlocky and tasteful, as well as handicrafts and ubiquitous carpet dealers, the streets of Sultanahmet await you.

WHAT TO BUY

Take your pick from an exhaustive range of beautiful ceramics (plates, bowls, İznik-style tiles), handicrafts (inlaid wood, alabaster ornaments), copperware, glassware, rich textiles (cotton, silk, cashmere, embroidered cloth, knitted goods, leather) and exquisite carpets and kilims. Blue glass-eye pendants, nargiles (bubble pipes) and miniature paintings are among the easiest and most affordable souvenirs, unless you want to take home a taste of Istanbul, in which case you simply can't beat fresh Turkish delight. Nuts in honey, halva, spices, raki or Turkish wine are also good choices.

USEFUL SHOPPING PHRASES

What time do the shops open/close?
Dükkanlar ne zaman açılır/kapanır?
Duekkanlar ne zaman acheler/kapanaer?

How much is this?
Kaça?
Kacha?

Can I try this on?
Bunu prova edebilir miyim?
Bunu prova edebilir miim?

My size is ...
Benim ölçüm ...
Benim oelchuem ...

I'll take this one, thank you.
Bunu alacağım, teşekkür ederim.
Bunu aladja'em, teshekkuer ederim.

This is too large/too small/too expensive.
Do you have any others?
Bu çok büyük/çok küçük/çok pahalı. Başka çeşitleriniz de var mı?
Bu chok bueyuek/chok kuechuek/chok paha'le. Bashka cheshitleriniz de var me?

Eating & drinking

Food and drink is everywhere in Istanbul and you will never have difficulty finding a restaurant or bar. The range of establishments is extensive, from low-cost *lokantas* (traditional Turkish restaurants) for quick meals to fine-dining restaurants for gourmets, and in between there are eateries, cafés and bars to suit most moods, budgets, taste buds and food fads. Turkish cuisine is rich and varied, as well as creative enough to successfully take on the fusion challenge, and at times it blends effortlessly with wider Mediterranean tastes.

Turkish starters, *mezes*, constitute the most creative aspect of Turkish food because there are endless variations and few hard and

● *Many eateries have a roof terrace*

fast rules about their composition. More often cold than hot, they are usually based around vegetables and fish and take the form of various purées and dips with yoghurt and salad ingredients. Served with fresh bread, a large plate of *mezes* can be a small meal in itself. *Börek* is another Turkish delicacy, a savoury and flaky pastry filled with anything from cheese with herbs to mince or vegetables. You may see them on a breakfast buffet, often cigar shaped. A *dolma* is any piece of food that can be filled with more food and some of the tastiest use vine leaves and peppers.

Drinking can be an equally eclectic experience and Turkish tastes take in tea (*çay*), herbal or straight, in neat little tulip-shaped glasses, black and strong coffee (*kahve*) in tiny cups, Turkish wines of reasonable quality, Turkey's own Efes Pilsen beer and anise-flavoured *raki*, which turns cloudy like absinthe when water is added.

Lunch is usually eaten between 12.30 and 14.00 and most restaurants open from around 11.00. Some will close around 15.00 and then open again in the evening, but most stay open all day. A tip of 10 per cent is normal and expected except in informal eateries of the self-service kind. Credit cards are generally accepted in most restaurants; look for the logos on the window or by the till.

TURKISH WINES

Doluca (D) and Kavaklıdere (K) are the two best-known Turkish wine estates. Çankaya (K) is a decent blend of four different grape varieties, as is the Villa Doluca red. Moskado (D) is from aromatic grapes, Kavak (K) is a standard, light white for fish, and Ancyra (K) is a fruity and aromatic red. Sarafin (D) is a stronger red. Both estates produce sparkling wines.

Picnic meals can be enjoyed during non-winter months in any of the city's parks and there is no shortage of small supermarkets and corner shops selling provisions. Fresh bread is best bought in the morning; look out for the street carts selling fresh *simit*, a ring-shaped savoury bread with sesame seeds. Fruit and vegetables are abundant except in winter, and there are many cheeses and dried meats to consider.

WHERE TO EAT

Where to go for a meal depends partly on what kind of experience you are seeking. For top-drawer dining with fine food from around

RESTAURANT RATINGS

Restaurant ratings in this book are based on the average price of a three-course dinner without drinks:

£ = Budget   ££ = Mid-range   £££ = Most expensive

the world – French or Japanese perhaps – and discerning wine lists, the 5-star hotels in the Taksim area should not disappoint. If you prefer to go for Turkish and international food, a rooftop terrace view of the Bosphorus and a romantic atmosphere, there are plenty of choices in the Beyoğlu, Karaköy or Ortaköy areas. Sultanahmet has its own crop of rooftop restaurants, many of which are remarkably affordable when you throw in stunning after-dark vistas of the Blue Mosque and Aya Sofya. Stylish, design-conscious restaurants are more likely to be found around Taksim and Beyoğlu than Sultanahmet or Galata.

The traditional Turkish restaurant is the *lokanta*, and usually serves pre-cooked food, which is kept warm in steel display tins.

Menus may not be in English but you can just point at what you'd like to try, take a risk, and be surprised; vegetarians can choose the obvious non-meat dishes and rice. Equally traditional are the meat-based kebab joints, *kebapçı* or *ocakbaşı*, and *pide* restaurants that serve a flat bread base with various toppings.

USEFUL DINING PHRASES

I would like a table for … people.
… kişilik bir masa istiyorum.
… kishilik beer masa istiyourum.

May I have the bill, please?   **Waiter/waitress!**
Hesap, lütfen?   Garson!
Hesap, lewtfen?   *Garson!*

Could I have it well-cooked/medium/rare, please?
İyice kızartılmış/normal/az pişmiş olsun lütfen?
Iyidje kezartelmesh/normal/az pishmish olsun lewtfen?

I am a vegetarian. Does this contain meat?
Ben vejeteryenım. Bu yiyecek et içeriyor mu?
Ben vejeteryen-aem. Boo yee-yecek et ee-cher-ee-yormoo?

Where is the toilet (restroom) please?
Tuvalet nerede acaba?
Tuvalet nerede adjaba?

I would like a cup of/two cups of/another coffee/tea.
Bir fincan/iki fincan/bir fincan daha kahve/çay istiyorum.
Beer findjan/eki findjan/beer findjan daha kahve/chai istiyourum.

Entertainment & nightlife

The Romans and Ottomans knew all about indulging the senses and having a good time and a new generation of young Istanbullas have created a lively and gregarious nightlife of their own. There are two neighbourhoods to know about and the one that is easiest to reach if staying in Sultanahmet is Beyoğlu, around Galata and down the side-streets off İstiklal Caddesi. Here, tucked away in narrow lanes, are smoky jazz clubs, chill-out bars and rooftop haunts where young professionals share a bottle of wine while gazing down at the twinkling lights of vessels in the Bosphorus darkness. The other area kicks into gear with the arrival of warm days in June and, sharing the understandable obsession for sea views, hugs the shoreline at Ortaköy. The scene is alfresco and more designer-conscious than Beyoğlu; the mood is Mediterranean but the wine and raki is pure Turkish. Less socially mixed than Beyoğlu, the air of affluence in Ortaköy is unmistakable.

In Sultanahmet itself the entertainment scene is more visitor-oriented and along Divan Yolu Caddesi, where hostels draw in

BE IN THE KNOW

Time Out Istanbul appears monthly (3.50 YTL) and there is an English edition with listings and reviews of the new bars and hottest clubs and restaurants in town. Here, too, are details of current exhibitions in the art galleries, reviews of the latest films and a wrap of the latest trends and trivia. Every two months, *The Guide* (5 YTL, but look for free copies in hotels) has a similar mix of articles and listings. It is like a *Yellow Pages* for the visitor, but is less discriminating than its rival.

backpackers, there is a string of pubs where the music pulsates until the early hours of the morning. Shows featuring Turkish belly dancing are usually as tacky as they sound and a good sing-along at a sociable restaurant like Kir Evi (see page 71) can be more fun.

CINEMA

April's International Istanbul Film Festival (see page 9) is testimony to the city's interest in films but at other times of the year, unless you speak Turkish, options are generally limited to Hollywood blockbusters and the occasional English success in their original language. It is always best to check at the box office when buying tickets, as some major releases may be dubbed into Turkish. There are plenty of cinemas, mostly on or around İstiklal Caddesi, and seats can and should be booked in advance at the box office. Credit cards are accepted, and the average price is 10 YTL or less, with discounts

● *Singer Asik Veysal (1843–1913) is remembered with a statue in Gülhane Parki*

sometimes for early screenings and for teachers or students (ID is not always required).

CULTURAL CENTRES

Theatre is nearly always performed in Turkish but the major cultural centres also host music, ballet and opera. Events featuring international orchestras are not uncommon and are by no means confined to Western European ones. Biletix (☎ 0216 454 1555 ⓦ www.biletix.com) is a central booking system for many events but sometimes it is better to turn up in advance and book your seat. The Atatürk Cultural Centre in Taksim Square is a major venue (☎ 0212 251 5600) and is home to the State Opera and Ballet, the Symphony Orchestra and the State Theatre Company. The box office is open daily from 10.00 to 18.00. For details of other venues and events, check one of the listings magazines. The Istanbul Foundation for Culture and Arts (☎ 0212 334 0700 ⓦ www.iksv.org/english) organizes the annual film, theatre and music festivals (see page 8).

FM RADIO STATIONS
Açık Radyo (94.9) rock, classical and folk
Capitol FM (99.5) pop and oldies
Metro FM (97.2) rock and pop
Radio Blue (94.5) jazz and latin-american
Radio Oxi-gen (95.9) acid-jazz and house
TRT3 (88.2) music and news broadcasts in English, French and German following Turkish news at 09.00, 12.00, 17.00 and 21.00

▶ *Many mosques have beautiful tiled walls*

Sport & relaxation

PARTICIPATION SPORTS
Swimming

Five-star hotels have swimming pools, gyms and saunas, but some have a nasty habit of charging guests for each visit. Free swimming can be enjoyed on a visit to Princes' Islands (see page 132) – if you can find a space – but don't even dip your toe in the polluted Bosphorus or the Golden Horn.

The *hamam* experience

Istanbul's perfect antidote for tired limbs and tourist fatigue, as well as being a cultural experience in its own right, is the *hamam*. A visit to a Turkish bath is up there with seeing the Topkapı Palace or the

● *Be pampered in one of the city's many bath-houses*

Blue Mosque but a lot more soothing on the body. Men and women have their own sections, modesty is preserved with towel wraps, and the process starts with a period of restful unwinding in a steam-filled hot room. There follow bouts of soaping and a vigorous exfoliating body scrub (a do-it-yourself ticket costs less but is also less fun), finished off with a body massage. The *hamam* experience is best enjoyed at the historic baths of Çemberlitaş (see page 73) or Cağaloğlu (see page 86), though a more private session is available at the Ambassador Hotel (see page 36).

SPECTATOR SPORTS

Soccer

The only sport that counts in Istanbul is soccer and it is not only the Bosphorus that divides Fenerbahçe, on the European side, from Galatasaray, over the water at Kadıköy. The rivalry is intense and, with Fenerbahçe claiming 25 million supporters across Turkey compared to Galatasaray's 4 or 5 million, a little one-sided. When either side achieves a notable victory, especially if chasing a European title, you will see and hear the crowds around Taksim Square. Tickets can be bought in advance at either stadium in the week preceding the game. There is a third Istanbul team, Beşiktaş, whose black and white colours contrast strongly with the yellow and blue of Fenerbahçe and the yellow and red of Galatasaray.

Beşiktaş Stadium ⓐ Spor Caddesi, Beşiktaş, close to Dolmabahçe Palace ⓣ 0212 227 8780 ⓝ Bus: T4 from Sultanahmet

Fenerbahçe Stadium ⓐ Kadıköy ⓣ 0216 345 0940 ⓦ www.fenerbahce.org.tr

Galatasaray Stadium ⓐ Galatasaray ⓣ 0212 251 5707 ⓦ www.galatasaray.org.tr

Accommodation

You should not have a problem finding somewhere to stay in Istanbul, whatever your budget and tastes, although the best deals will be snapped up in summer and advance internet booking is advisable. Use hotels' websites wherever possible. Other useful websites include www.istanbul.com and, for reservations, www.istanbulreservation.com. For hostels and the least expensive accommodation options, www.hostelbookers.com is a good site. Prices are sometimes quoted in euros.

Sultanahmet, the centre for sightseeing, has a concentration of affordable accommodation, including hostels, plus some attractive hotels. Across the Golden Horn in Beyoğlu you will find a selection of mid-range hotels and, because of the area's 19th-century history, there is some character to the place as well as easy access to İstiklal Caddesi and to Galata Bridge for Sultanahmet. At the top end of İstiklal Caddesi, in and around Taksim Square, the top-notch, brand-name hotels cluster and provide 5-star accommodation.

Hotels are categorised by the government using a 1-star to 5-star rating and there is also another category for one-off 'Special' hotels, earned as a result of the historic status of their buildings. This category does not reflect service or amenities, but room rates often match 4- and 5-star places even though the facilities may be restricted by preservation orders. What you do get is a unique experience, and advance booking is essential in high season.

Room rates, which usually include a buffet breakfast, tend to be seasonally adjusted and the higher rates apply to the April–October period and the Christmas/New Year break. Do not be timid about bargaining for a discount, especially if you are staying more than one night, and if a sea view is important, clarify this before confirming your booking. It is often the case, though not with 5-star hotels, that a 10 per cent discount or more will be given if you pay in cash rather than by credit card. There is a hotel-booking desk at the airport but avoid this if you can because the rates are predatory.

All the hotels listed here are comfortable, well-run establishments and, apart from dorm beds in hostels, the rooms come with en-suite bathroom and air-conditioning. Televisions are standard but only cable or satellite service provides English-language news programmes.

For hotels on the Asian side of the Bosphorus and on the Bosphorus coastline, see page 139.

SULTANAHMET

Istanbul Hostel £ Not as noisy as some of the nearby hostels, a pleasant atmosphere, rooftop terrace and downstairs bar. ⓐ Kutlugün Sokak 35 ⓣ 0212 516 9380 ⓦ www.hostelbookers.com

Sultan Hostel £–££ Dorms and singles, and doubles nudging into ££, café, outdoor bar with good views, free use of internet. ⓐ Akbiyik Caddesi 21 ⓣ 0212 516 9260 ⓕ 0212 516 9262 ⓦ www.sultanhostel.com

---

ACCOMMODATION RATINGS

Accommodation ratings in this book are based on the average price of a room for two people between April and October for one night, including tax and breakfast unless otherwise stated:

£ Budget   under 50 YTL
££ Mid-range   between 50 and 100 YTL
£££ Expensive   over 100 YTL

Alp ££ Smart-looking hotel, well-run, with safety boxes, cable TV, and a fridge to keep your drinks before bringing them up to the rooftop bar for views of the Bosphorus. ⓐ Akbiyik Caddesi, Adliye Sokak 4 ⓣ 0212 517 7067 ⓕ 0212 517 9570 ⓦ www.alpguesthouse.com

Ayasofya ££ Comfortable, faded elegance; not to be confused with the more expensive Ayasofya Pansiyonlari. ⓐ Demirci Reşit Sokak 28, Küçük Ayasofya Caddesi ⓣ 0212 516 9446 ⓕ 0212 518 0770 ⓦ www.ayasofyahotel.com

Hanedan ££ Same management as the Alp and Peninsula and an equally well-run establishment with its own roof terrace. ⓐ Akbiyik Caddesi, Adliye Sokak 3 ⓣ 0212 516 4869 ⓕ 0212 458 2248 ⓦ www.hanedanhotel.com

Peninsula ££ Roof terrace, functional rooms but friendly management and airport pick-up for 12 YTL. ⓐ Akbiyik Caddesi, Adliye Sokak 6 ⓣ 0212 458 6850 ⓕ 0212 458 6849 ⓦ www.hotelpeninsula.com

Şebnem ££ Family-run, friendly guesthouse with small but tasteful rooms and superb sea views from the rooftop. ⓐ Adliye Sokak 1 ⓣ 0212 215 517 6623 ⓕ 0212 638 1056 ⓦ www.sebnemhotel.com

Ambassador £££ Great location, facilities include a *hamam* and direct bookings include airport pick-up and breakfast on the rooftop terrace. ⓐ Ticarethane Sokak 19 ⓣ 0212 511 9828 ⓕ 0212 512 0005 ⓦ www.ambassador.com

Ayasofya Pansiyonlari £££ Ottoman-style boutique hotel with Special status and a picturesque location next door to Topkapı Palace. ⓐ Soğukçeşme Sokak ⓣ 0212 513 3660 ⓦ www.ayasofyapansiyonlari.com

Eresin Crown Hotel £££ Elegant, well-run, minutes from the sights and an above-average restaurant to boot. ⓐ Küçük Ayasofya Caddesi 40 ⓣ 0212 638 4428 ⓕ 0212 638 0933 ⓦ www.eresincrown.com.tr

Sarnic £££ Boutique-ish feel to this 16-room hotel with rooftop breakfast and good restaurant. ⓐ Küçük Ayasofya Caddesi 26 ⓣ 0212 518 2323 ⓕ 0212 518 2414 ⓦ www.sarnichotel.com

🔺 *A decorative feature for the Eresin Crown Hotel lobby*

BEYOĞLU

Galata Residence Camono Apart Hotel ££ Large rooms with kitchens, no breakfast, and an authentic sense of living in old Istanbul. ⓐ Banakalar Caddesi, Hacı Ali Sokak, Galata ⓣ 0212 252 6062 ⓕ 0212 244 2323 ⓦ www.galataresidence.com

Gulsa ££ Small rooms but clean and centrally located. No breakfast. ⓐ İstiklal Caddesi, Acara Sokak 7, Galatasaray ⓣ 0212 251 6171 ⓕ 0212 244 2927 ⓦ hotelgulsa@mynet.com

Anemon Galata £££ Next to the Galata Tower, this Special category hotel has a terrace café and gloriously classical décor. ⓐ Bereketzade Mahallesi Büyükhendek Caddesi 11 ⓣ 0212 293 2343 ⓕ 0212 292 2340 ⓦ www.anemonhotels.com

Pera Palas £££ Museum-like hotel where Agatha Christie stayed and wrote *Murder on the Orient Express* in room 411. ⓐ Meşrutiyet Caddesi 98–100 ⓣ 0212 251 4560 ⓕ 0212 251 4089 ⓦ www.perapalas.com

Richmond £££ In the heart of the city, with sea or city views and good eating possibilities. ⓐ İstiklal Caddesi 445 ⓣ 0212 252 5460 ⓕ 0212 252 977 ⓦ www.richmondhotels.com

TAKSIM

Marmara £££ Landmark hotel with grand views, 5-star service and a busy atmosphere; confirm whether breakfast is included when booking. ⓐ Taksim Square ⓣ 0212 251 4696 ⓕ 0212 244 0509 ⓦ www.themarmaraistanbul.com

Point Hotel £££ Nearly 200 rooms, wireless internet and DVD players in the rooms, views of the Bosphorus. ⓐ Topçu Caddesi Taksim Square ⓣ 0212 313 5000 ⓕ 0212 313 5030 ⓦ www.pointhotel.com

Swissôtel The Bosphorus £££ Stylish, 5-star hotel with excellent facilities. Close to Taksim Square but awkward to reach on foot; easy with taxis. ⓐ Bayıdım Caddesi 2 ⓣ 0212 326 1100 ⓕ 0212 326 1122 ⓦ www.swissotel.com

⬤ Some market stalls come to you – like this bread-seller

THE BEST OF ISTANBUL

Istanbul is so awash with cultural treasures and apparently must-see sights that a first-time visitor can feel overwhelmed. It's a good idea to work out your priorities; if you become enamoured with the city there will always be a return trip. Ticking off visits to postcard sights will exhaust you, and you will probably have a more enjoyable time if you take it easy, find some time to wander and allow for Turkish serendipity.

TOP 10 ATTRACTIONS

* **Mosques** Not all of them, but the Blue Mosque (see page 64) and Süleymaniye Camıı (see page 78) are two of the most impressive and beautiful.

* **Topkapı Palace and Harem** Principal residence and pleasure palace of the Ottoman sultans (see page 66).

* **Aya Sofya** The largest enclosed space for over a millennium (see page 64).

* **Pummelling pleasures at a *hamam*** Tension and fatigue scrubbed and massaged away in an ancient steam bath. The best are Çemberlitaş (see page 73) and Cağaloğlu (see page 86).

- **Cruising the Bosphorus** Straddle Europe and Asia with a trip up the Bosphorus (see pages 116–118).

- **Buzzing bazaars** The hyper-real Spice Bazaar (see page 78) and, if want your bazaar experience on a mega scale, the Grand Bazaar (see page 76) as well.

- **Jazzy moments at the Nardis Jazz Club** (see page 99) Best enjoyed after a meal in the nearby converted prison (see page 97).

- **Afternoon tea at Pera Palas Hotel** Time travel to the 1890s (see page 38).

- **Cocktails over the Bosphorus** From one of the many rooftop terrace restaurants in Beyoğlu.

- **The Istanbul Modern and the Pera Museum** Contemporary art at the city's hottest galleries (see page 92).

▼ *The Blue Mosque is one of the city's best assets*

Your brief guide to seeing and experiencing the best of Istanbul, depending on the time you have available.

HALF-DAY: ISTANBUL IN A HURRY

It would be a mad rush to see both sides of the Golden Horn; by staying in Sultanahmet you can explore this historic side and enjoy a walk beginning at the Blue Mosque. Even a quick visit inside will reveal its splendour and the same could be done for nearby Aya Sofya, best reached by walking through Arasta Bazaar for some shopping on the hoof. From here it is five minutes to a tram stop on

● *The most elegant-looking surgery: the Circumcision Room at Topkapı Palace*

Divan Yolu Caddesi – cafés, restaurants and bars here offer refreshment – buy a ticket at the booth and hop on a tram for a short ride to Eminönü. Here you will see the Golden Horn and sense the majesty of the city and, if there is still time, pop into the nearby Spice Bazaar for some oriental razzmatazz.

1 DAY: TIME TO SEE A LITTLE MORE

The half-day itinerary above could easily stretch into a day's activity just by slowing down the pace. The extra time would also allow for a Turkish bath at Çemberlitaş before boarding a tram to Eminönü. Alternatively, instead of a *hamam*, the Galata Bridge can be crossed on foot, by tram or taxi, or take your lunch at one of the many restaurants underneath it while gazing at the busy sea traffic. There might still be time to take in the Istanbul Modern, five minutes by taxi from the other side of Galata Bridge.

2–3 DAYS: SHORT CITY-BREAK

The first day, or day and a half, could be occupied with the suggestions above, while the extra time would allow for a visit to Topkapı Palace and its harem, some leisurely shopping in the byways off İstiklal Caddesi and/or a trip up the Bosphorus. There would also be time to think about after-dark entertainment by way of a rooftop restaurant overlooking the Bosphorus, a bar or club to unwind in or, in summer, a taxi out to Ortaköy for one of the chic, waterside restaurants.

LONGER: ENJOYING ISTANBUL TO THE FULL

Once you have enjoyed all of the above, you will have time to experience the full Top Ten. After all that, you will really appreciate that Turkish bath.

Something for nothing

Sultanahmet's cityscape at night is there for the taking and the lit-up exteriors of the Blue Mosque and Aya Sofya are an experience in themselves. Even a very small donation will cover a visit to the Blue Mosque. No one minds if you wander into the period-piece Pera Palas Hotel, pretending you have just stepped off the Orient Express, or, with the famous train in mind, visit the free Orient Express museum at the railway station. Every Thursday, 10.00–14.00, entrance to the Istanbul Modern is free and the often exceptional exhibitions at the Pera Museum are always free.

For the small price of a ticket on the ferry (2 YTL each way), an evening could be enjoyed by taking one of the regular boats from Eminönü to Kadıköy. Along the way you will experience the splendour of the Bosphorus and the city at night. Disembarking at Kadıköy (don't get off at the first stop; see page 130), you step foot in Asia and the atmosphere can be soaked up on a short walk before catching a boat back.

Beyoğlu and Taksim are full of temptations for your credit card but walk for free into Çukurcuma by going down Sıraselviler Caddesi from Taksim Square. Five minutes down this road, follow the signs pointing right to Galatasaray and Karaköy. You enter Ağa Hamami Caddesi and follow the next sign to Galatasaray by turning right at the Or-Ka store and then take the first left downhill, passing Evi Han and Leyla (see page 109). Follow the street down, turn left and take the first right at the Ottoman shop and then left again. The street is full of little galleries and the architecture of old Istanbul. At the bottom, go left into Hayriye Caddesi and follow it around. Walk through the entrance to French St and its restaurants on your right and up the steps at the other end. Turn left here and then right onto

Yeni Carsi Caddesi with its bookshops, one of which has an
inexpensive downstairs café. This street leads onto İstiklal Caddesi
and a right turn returns you to Taksim Square.

◗ *International art exhibitions for free, uniquely, at the Pera Museum*

When it rains

Nine of the Top Ten attractions are not dependent on fine weather; only the enjoyment of a cruise up the Bosphorus relies on a fine day. The Blue Mosque and Süleymaniye Camıı, as well as Aya Sofya, need to be appreciated from the outside, especially after dark, but once inside you are protected from the elements. The rooms of Topkapı Palace and the harem tour are all weather-proof and many hours could be spent wandering the covered Grand Bazaar. A wet day is the ideal time to benefit from a Turkish bath because you can spend as much time as you like in the steam room and linger restfully over a drink after the experience before leaving the *hamam*.

Two historically important attractions that would make a Top Twelve list are the Basilica Cistern and Dolmabahçe Palace, and both these places are impervious to the weather. Museums, of course, are ideal places when it rains and the Archaeological Museum and the adjoining Museum of the Ancient Orient could easily occupy half a day. There are also a number of smaller museums that might not grab your attention when the sun shines but are worthy of your time if the subject matter appeals. Strong contenders are the Museum of Turkish and Islamic Arts and the Military Museum, and not to be forgotten is the small Orient Express museum at the railway station. The station has the atmospheric Orient Express restaurant and a café extension onto one of the platforms, and there is a period charm to enjoy while sipping a drink and watching the railway traffic.

By way of entertainment, the cinemas of Istanbul suggest themselves as a way of escaping the rain and, before or after, a leisurely drink and/or meal is always to be had in one or more of the numerous cafés, bars or restaurants in Beyoğlu or around Taksim, the areas where most of the cinemas are located. Spending longer than you might otherwise have planned in a café or bar is a great way to find yourself chatting to Istanbullas and enjoying their company.

🔺 *Keep dry at the Orient Express Museum*

On arrival

TIME DIFFERENCES

Istanbul time is two hours ahead of Greenwich Mean Time (GMT) but between the end of March and the end of October clocks are put forward an hour and this puts Istanbul time three hours ahead of GMT. In mid-summer in Turkey at 12.00 noon, times elsewhere are as follows:

Australia Eastern Standard Time 19.00, Central Standard Time 18.30, Western Standard Time 17.00
New Zealand 21.00
South Africa 11.00
UK 10.00
USA and Canada Newfoundland Time 06.30, Atlantic Canada Time 06.00, Eastern Time 05.00, Central Time 04.00, Mountain Time 03.00, Pacific Time 02.00, Alaska 01.00

ARRIVING
By air
Atatürk International Airport (www.ataturkairport.com) is 23 km (14 miles) west of Sultanahmet, the old part of Istanbul, and has all the facilities you would expect, including ATMs, a 24-hour tourist information office and left luggage facility.

Buses from the airport: The Havaş airport bus departs from outside the arrivals hall and takes about 45 minutes to reach Taksim Square. It is the cheapest option for getting into the city and costs 8.5 YTL. Along the way, it stops at Aksaray and from here a taxi or a tram could be taken to Sultanahmet. The return bus departs from outside the Havaş ticket office on Cumhuriyet Caddesi, just off Taksim Square, every half hour between 05.00 and 23.00.

Light railway from the airport: The light rail system travels from the airport to Aksaray, from where you can take a taxi or tram to Sultanahmet. You can also reach Sultanahmet by taking the light rail train to Zeytinburnu, the sixth stop and the beginning of a tram line that runs eastwards to Sultanahmet. The transfer from rail to tram at Zeytinburnu is easier than transferring at Aksaray and, being the beginning of the tram line, makes travel with luggage easier.

⬥ *Istanbul time: two or three hours ahead of Greenwich Mean Time (GMT)*

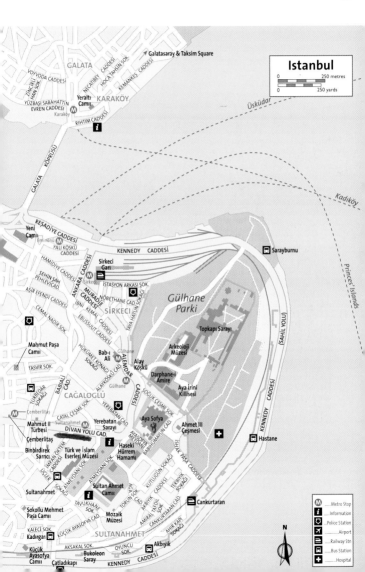

Istanbul

| 0 | 250 metres |
| 0 | 250 yards |

GALATA

Galatasaray & Taksim Square

VOYVODA CADDESI
ZİNCİRLİ HAN SOK.
YÜZBAŞI SABAHATTİN EVREN CADDESİ
NECATİBEY CADDESİ
HOCA TAHSIN SOK.
KEMANKEŞ CADDESİ

Yeraltı Camii

KARAKÖY

Karaköy
RIHTIM CADDESİ

Üsküdar

Kadıköy

Princes' Islands

GALATA KÖPRÜSÜ

REŞADİYE CADDESİ
Yeni Camii
Eminönü
YALI KÖŞKÜ CADDESİ

KENNEDY CADDESİ

Sarayburnu

HAMİDİYE CADDESİ
ŞEHİN ŞAH PEHLEVİ CAD.
ANKARA CADDESİ
Sirkeci Garı
Sirkeci
İSTASYON ARKASI SOK.
MURADİYE CADDESİ
İBNİ KEMAL CADDESİ
NÖBETHANE CAD.
TAYA HATUN SOKAĞI

Gülhane Parkı

AŞİR EFENDİ CADDESİ
SİRKECİ
EBUSSUUT CADDESİ

Topkapı Sarayı

CEMAL NADİR SOK.

(SAHİL YOLU)

Mahmut Paşa Camii

Arkeoloji Müzesi

KENNEDY CADDESİ

HÜKÜMET KONAĞI SOKAĞI
Bab-ı Ali
Gülhane
Alay Köşkü

Darphane-i Amire

TASVİR SOK.
BABIALİ CAD.
ALEMDAR CADDESİ
ALAYKÖŞKÜ CAD.

Aya İrini Kilisesi

TÜRBEDAR SOKAĞI
ÇAĞALOĞLU
Gülhane
SOĞUK ÇEŞME SOK.

Çemberlitaş
ÇATAL ÇEŞME SOK.
YEREBATAN CAD.

Ahmet III Çeşmesi

Hastane

Mahmut II Türbesi
Sultanahmet
DİVAN YOLU CAD.
Yerebatan Sarayı

Çemberlitaş
Aya Sofya

BABIHÜMAYUN CAD.

Binbirdirek Sarnıcı
Türk ve İslam Eserleri Müzesi
Haseki Hürrem Hamamı

İMRAN ÖKTEM CAD.
KLODFARER CAD.
ATMEYDANI SOK.
AYASOFYA MEYDANI

Sultanahmet
ÜÇLER SOK.
KUTLUGÜN SOKAĞI
TERBIYIK SOKAĞI

Sokollu Mehmet Paşa Camii
Sultan Ahmet Camii
AÇIK CAD.
ARTIK HADIM CADDESİ
ARTIK HADIM CAD.
AMİRAL TAFDİL CAD.
CANKURTARAN CAD.

TAVUKHANE SOK.
TORUN SOK.

Cankurtaran

KALECİ SOK.
Kadırgalı
Mozaik Müzesi

KÜÇÜK AYASOFYA CAD.
AHIR KAPI SOKAĞI

Küçük Ayasofya Camii
Catladıkapı
AKSAKAL SOK.
OYUNCU SOK.
Bukoleon Saray
Akbıyık

SULTANAHMET
KENNEDY CADDESİ

N

Ⓜ	Metro Stop
🛈	Information
Ⓞ	Police Station
✈	Airport
🚆	Railway Stn
🚌	Bus Station
✚	Hospital

Taxis from the airport: Taxis to Taksim or Sultanahmet cost about £17/€25 and are available from outside the arrivals hall.

Transport maps and more details can be found at http://www.turkeyplanner.com/wheretogo/istanbul

By rail
Long-distance trains from Europe arrive at Sirkeci Station, in the heart of the city, next to Eminönü, and tram and bus stops for Sultanahmet and Taksim Square.

🔺 Hop on the antique tram for a ride in modern Istanbul

By road

Nothing is gained by driving in Istanbul; the traffic is dense and parking spaces are extremely scarce in this city that is so easy to get around by public transport and taxis.

FINDING YOUR FEET

Istanbul can be a confusing place when first setting out to travel across the city but it takes only a short while to adjust to the public transport systems and learn the ropes. If coming from the UK, because driving is on the right, watch out when crossing roads. Wherever you come from, beware of vehicular traffic because indicators are infrequently used and pedestrian rights is a fanciful notion for many drivers.

IF YOU GET LOST, TRY ...

Excuse me, do you speak English?
Afedersiniz, İngilizce biliyor musunuz?
Afedersiniz, engilizdje biliyor musunuz?

Excuse me, is this the right way to ... the cathedral/the tourist office/the castle/the old town?
Afedersiniz, ... 'e/a/ye/ya buradan mı gidilir ... Katedral/turist enformasyon bürosu/şato/eski şehir?
Afedersiniz, ... 'e/a/ye/ya buradan me gidilir ... Cathedral/tourist enformasyon buerosu/shato/eski shehir?

Can you point to it on my map?
Haritamın üzerinde gösterebilir misiniz?
Haritamaen uezerinde goesterebilir misiniz?

ORIENTATION

Istanbul is divided by a narrow strait of water, the Bosphorus, which also divides Europe from Asia and this creates a European and an Asian half to the city. The Golden Horn is an inlet of water that feeds into the Bosphorus from the European side and this divides European Istanbul itself into two areas: Sultanahmet, the old city where most of the historical sites are to be found, and the more modern metropolis centred around İstiklal and Taksim Square. While most of your sightseeing time will be spent in and around Sultanahmet, it is the other side of the Golden Horn that boasts a concentration of restaurants, bars and clubs.

The Galata Bridge is the most usual route you will use for crossing between Sultanahmet and Taksim. From the Taksim side of the bridge, the Tünel funicular railway will take you in seconds uphill to Beyoğlu. This is the elegant 19th-century quarter of European Istanbul and its main boulevard, İstiklal Caddesi, runs up to Taksim Square.

Beyond Taksim, to the northeast and on the shore of the Bosphorus, are the neighbourhoods of Beşiktaş and Ortaköy. These areas have attractions of their own and a host of entertainment possibilities by way of drinking, eating and clubbing.

Across the Bosphorus, on the Asian side of Istanbul, the main centres where you are likely to spend time are Kadıköy and Üsküdar.

GETTING AROUND

It is possible to travel on foot between most of the principal attractions in Sultanahmet and many of them will be within walking distance of your accommodation if you are based in this part of the city. Topkapı Palace, Aya Sofya and the Blue Mosque – the three major sights – are conveniently close to one another, and

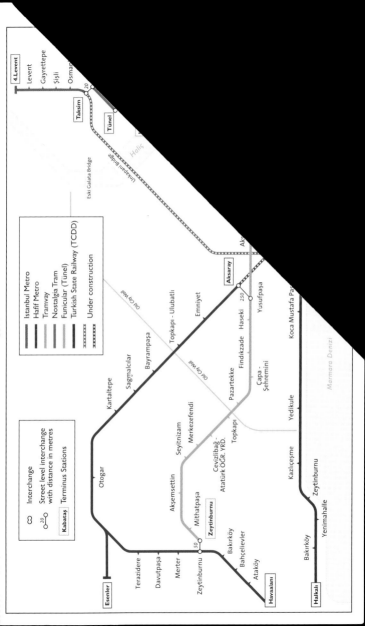

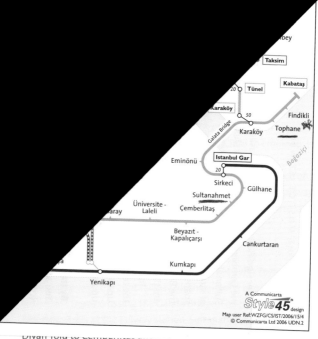

A Communicarta
Style**45** design
Map user Ref:WZFG/CS/IST/2006/15/4
© Communicarta Ltd 2006 UDN.2

bought from the booths at any of the stops and, for the old trams on İstiklal Caddesi that run between Tünel and Taksim without stopping, at kiosks at either end of the line. Tram tickets cost less than 1 YTL.

By bus

The service you are most likely to use is the very useful T4 green-coloured bus that runs between Sultanahmet, from behind the tourist office, to Taksim Square, stopping along the way in Karaköy, just over the Galata Bridge, and near Dolmabahçe Palace. Tickets are purchased before boarding from booths near main bus stations like Taksim and Eminönü, or from private vendors for a small mark-up; buy two if planning a return journey. Bus tickets cost less than 1 YTL.

The Tünel

This funicular railway climbs the steep uphill journey of 500 m (550 yds) from Karaköy to Tünel Square in Beyoğlu, the start/end of İstiklal Caddesi. Tokens are bought from the booth at the entrance and cost less than 1 YTL.

By taxi

Licensed taxis, bright yellow in colour and relatively inexpensive, are everywhere and can be hailed on the street. Fares are digitally metered but always check that the meter reads *gündüz* (daytime) for rides between 06.00 and 24.00; if it reads *gece* (night-time) you will be paying 50 per cent more. The bridge toll will be added to your fare if crossing one of the Bosphorus bridges. Tipping is not expected although rounding up the fare to the nearest lira is common. Meters on taxis start at 1.5 YTL and then clock up 1 YTL for every kilometre during daytime; night-time rates start at 2.5 YTL and then 1.5 YTL per kilometre.

By boat

Boats travel constantly up and down the Bosphorus and across it to Kadıköy and Üsküdar. The principal terminus is at Eminönü. Boats also depart from Karaköy, just across the Galata Bridge and opposite Eminönü, but not from here for the Bosphorus cruises. All piers are clearly marked with their destinations and you purchase your ticket from the nearby booths. Boats to Kadıköy and Üsküdar cost just over 1 YTL and a single ticket for travel up the Bosphorus is around 2 YTL.

By metro

The metro system is still being built and although some lines are in operation, you are unlikely to use them because they serve the suburbs and do not access Istanbul's main attractions.

THE AKBIL TRAVEL PASS

The Akbil system saves time and some money if you staying for more than a few days. It uses a metal tag, accepted electronically on trams, buses, light railway and metro, and is bought at main stations (including Zeytinburnu if you are coming from the airport). There is a refundable deposit for the metal tag and its value can be updated as and when it becomes necessary.

🔽 *View of the Topkapı Palace with boats on the river*

▶ *Light up your day with a visit to a craft shop*

Sultanahmet

Sultanahmet is small and compact, relatively traffic-free compared to the rest of the city and an area you can easily find your way around on foot. The sights below are ordered on the basis of an extended walking tour that begins outside Topkapı Palace; be prepared for some persistent, if polite, carpet-shop touts along the way.

SIGHTS & ATTRACTIONS *1*

Outside Topkapı Sarayı (Topkapı Palace)

At the corner of Babi-I Hümayun Caddesi and Soğuk Çeşme Sokak stands the early 18th-century Fountain of Ahmet III (Ahmet Cesmesi), a suitably elegant approach to the picturesque Soğuk Çeşme Sokak and its traditional painted houses. To enter the first courtyard of the palace, freely walk through the imperial Gate in front of the fountain, passing the 6th-century Byzantine church of Haghia Eirene (which was never converted into a mosque). The twin-towered entrance to the Palace is straight ahead but veer left to bypass it and check out the entrance to the Archaeological Museum and the way into Gülhane Park.

Gülhane Parki (Gülhane Park) *2*

Once the sultans' private palace park, this area of green offers welcome relief from the hustle and bustle in and around the palace. As well as offering a picnic site in the shade, there is a tea garden and, if you walk northeast and cross Kennedy Caddesi, a viewing point for the meeting of the Golden Horn and the Bosphorus. You will need to retrace your steps to leave the park onto Alemadar Caddesi and the Gülhane stop on the tram line.

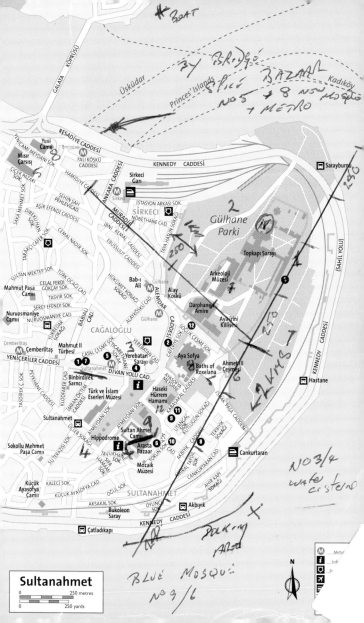

Yerebatan Sarayı (Basilica Cistern)

Close to where Alemadar Caddesi meets Yerebatan Caddesi
is the entrance to the largest underground cistern in the city,
the Basilica Cistern (Yerebatan Sarayı Muzesi), built to supply
water for the palace area under Justinian in AD 532. The roof
is held up by 12 rows of 28 columns, with each column over 8 m
(26 ft) high. Two of the columns rest on bases that are shaped
into Medusa heads.

ⓐ Yerebatan Caddesi 1 ☎ 0212 522 1259 ⏰ 09.30–19.30 (summer);
09.30–17.30 (winter); admission charge

Hippodrome

Ok, you have to imagine the massed crowds rising to their feet in
Byzantium's greatest stadium as rival chariot teams gallop towards
the finishing line, but inside the Hippodrome, now a public space,
open 24 hours, you do have the sense of a grand, linear space – the
stadium was enlarged by Constantine to hold as many as 100,000 –
and some suitably ancient monuments in situ to help create the
scene. Constantine brought the **Egyptian Obelisk**, dated 1500 BC,
which stands on a base from the 4th century. He also shipped over
from Delphi the 5th-century **Serpentine Column**, which stands
next to it, while the third, dilapidated-looking monument has an
unknown provenance, though it is known to have been restored
by a 10th-century emperor.

Baths of Roxelana

This two-domed structure was built in the mid-15th century as the
baths for worshippers at nearby Aya Sofya and named after the wife
of the sultan, Süleyman the Magnificent, under whose orders it was
built. The building is now a government-run carpet and kilim shop,

but visitors are free to wander in and admire the bath's original features which are still intact.

ⓐ Aya Sofya Square 4 ⓣ 0212 513 8458 ⓛ 10.00–18.00 Mon–Sat, closed Sun

Çemberlitaş

Known also as Constantine's Column, this elegant porphyry column was brought from Egypt in AD 330 as part of the city's new status as the capital of the Byzantine empire. It has been restored a number of times, most recently in 2006, though no one is thinking of re-topping it with a replacement statue of the emperor that originally adorned its summit. The column is open to view, free of charge, and just to the side of it is the entrance to the historic Çemberlitaş *hamam*; go on, take a peep and decide – can you leave Istanbul without taking a bath?

ⓐ Vezir Hanı Caddesi 8

CULTURE

Arkeoloji Müzesi (Archaeological Museum and the Museum of the Ancient Orient)

Between them, these two museums, covered by the one entrance ticket, contain a large collection of works of art and artefacts from ancient Greece and Rome as well as priceless treasures from pre-classical civilisations. There is far too much to list here, but try not to miss the carved marble tomb depicting Persian forces being defeated by Alexander the Great, the world' earliest surviving peace treaty (1269 BC) providing for the mutual release of political prisoners, and the animal relief from the time of Nebuchadnezzar in Babylon.

ⓐ Osman Hamdi Bey Yokuşu, Gülhane ⓣ 0212 520 7740

ⓛ 09.00–17.30 Tues–Sun, closed Mon; admission charge

Aya Sofya

The 'Church of Holy Wisdom', also known by its Greek name Haghia Sophia, was built by Emperor Justinian in the 6th century AD and after 916 years was converted into a mosque after the Ottomans conquered the city. In 1935 it was converted into a museum – so no arguments over its theological identity – while its world significance remains undisputed in terms of monumental architecture. The dome is 30 m (32 yds) in diameter, supported by 40 brick-built ribs that depend on four colossal pillars for their stability. Apart from the remarkably absorbing silence of the vast, domed space, there are fine mosaics and marbles which are not easily seen in the poor light.

ⓐ Aya Sofya Square **ⓣ** 0212 522 098 **ⓛ** 09.00–17.00 Tues–Sun, closed Mon; admission charge

Sultan Ahmet Camıı (Blue Mosque)

Taking its name from the characteristically blue İznik tiles that decorate the interior, the famous Blue Mosque (Sultan Ahmet Camıı) can prove more soul-stirring from the outside, especially at night when it is lit up and shines serenely with a strange self-possession. Built in the early 17th century, the construction plans aroused controversy because it was apparently thought that a mosque with six minarets would sacrilegiously challenge the supremacy of the mosque at Mecca. Unlike Aya Sofya, the interior is flooded with natural light. There is a free sound and light show from May to September from 19.30 outside the mosque.

ⓐ Hippodrome **ⓣ** 0212 518 1319 **ⓛ** 08.30–16.30 (but avoid visiting during Friday prayers)

ⓞ *Natural light floods the interior of Aya Sofya*

Türk ve İslam Eserleri Müzesi (Museum of Turkish & Islamic Art)

An excellent space with an artful and discerning collection of Islamic works of art housed in a graceful old Ottoman residence restored in 1843, the museum has survived largely unaltered into the 21st century. The exhibits are richly varied: Persian miniatures, Turkish carpets, works of highly wrought calligraphy, paintings and ethnographic displays. There is a nice little shop, too, for cards and small mats.

ⓐ Hippodrome ❶ 0212 518 1805 ⏱ 09.00–16.30 Tues–Sun, closed Mon; admission charge

Topkapı Sarayı (Topkapı Palace)

The *numero uno* visitor attraction, a been-there-and-bought-the-t-shirt kind of place, Topkapı Palace is yet undeniably difficult to resist and especially so when you have to enter it to access the harem. The palace was the administrative and erotic centre for the rulers of the Ottoman empire from 1465 to 1853 and there is a lot to see on one visit; you may want to just pick out some of the highlights and reserve some energy and interest for the tour of the harem. The **treasury** is as full of glittering riches as you would expect and includes the emerald-decorated **Topkapı Dagger**, featured in the Peter Ustinov classic *Topkapı*, and the **Spoonmaker's Diamond** which, if you believe the blarney, was bought for three spoons from a junk merchant. The **Circumcision Room** has a most attractive exterior of İznik tiles from the 16th and 17th centuries. Before you leave the palace, seek out the last building built in the complex; it is now the Konyali Café (see page 70), and even if you don't eat or drink, the panoramic views from the terrace are worth admiring.

ⓐ Soğuk Çeşme Sokak ❶ 0212 512 0480 ⏱ 09.00–17.00 Mon & Wed–Sun, closed Tues; admission charge

Topkapı Harem

The first stop on the mandatory tour is the **Court of the Black Eunuchs**, the harem's guards, before proceeding to the luxurious rooms of the valide sultan (see page 12). As you continue, some of the many highlights include the decorous dining room of the fruit-and-floral-loving Ahmet III and the over-the-top sumptuous luxury of Murat III's chamber. It is up to you to imagine the debauchery and licence indulged in by the sultans, although the sober fact is that the harem was the living quarters for a sizeable community of people and not – well, not always – the venue for decadent orgies. That was what the Romans did.

ⓐ Topkapı Palace, Soğuk Çeşme Sokak ⓔ 09.00–17.00 Mon & Wed–Sun, closed Tues, guided tours every 30 minutes 09.30–16.00; separate admission charge at the entrance inside Topkapı Palace

RETAIL THERAPY

Azim Dağitim Down a left turn if walking between the Çemberlitaş and Beyazıt tram stops, this shop has an interesting selection of Turkish folk music, like Neyzen Teyfit, plus Sufi and Dervish instrumental albums. ⓐ Klodfarer Caddesi 6 ⓣ 0212 638 1313 ⓦ www.azimdagitim ⓔ 09.00–20.00, closed Sun (summer); 09.00–19.00, closed Sun (winter)

Carpet Café There are so many carpet shops in Sultanahmet – and so many scams, one suspects – that singling one out could be a reckless enterprise. At least, though, in this shop there is no hard sell and the carpets and rugs are of some quality. Having said that, shop around and judge for yourself. ⓐ Alemdar Caddesi 22 ⓣ 0212 519 6289 ⓦ www.carpet-cafe.com ⓔ 08.00–20.00

Doruk Leather Centre Opposite the Magnaura restaurant (see page 72), this supermarket-like store caters for men and women. Ask for a discount and haggle if necessary for at least 30 per cent off the marked price. ⓐ Akbıyık Caddesi 28–30 ⓣ 0212 458 0770 ⓛ 09.00–19.00

Dösimm Passed on your way to the Topkapı Palace ticket office, inside the first courtyard, this government-run handicraft store has the special virtue of fixed prices. A kiosk by the shop's entrance sells stamps and phone cards. ⓐ Babi-I Hümayun Caddesi, Topkapı Palace ⓣ 0212 513 3134 ⓛ 09.00–17.00

Galeri Cengiz One of the many small shops in Arasta Bazaar, parallel to the Hippodrome but behind the Blue Mosque, selling embroidered bags, shoes and boots using materials from Uzbekistan and Turkmenistan. ⓐ Arasta Bazaar 157 ⓣ 0212 518 8882 ⓛ 09.00–19.00

Gift Land Easy to find, situated on one of Sultanahmet's main visitor-oriented streets full of restaurants and bars, and unpretentiously offering just what the shop's name suggests. Come here for ceramics, paintings, carpets and, well, gifts. ⓐ Akbıyık Caddesi 51 ⓣ 0212 518 4434 ⓛ 09.00–22.00

Inkat Uçan The easiest way to find this book and music shop is to follow the way into Topkapı Palace from Gülhane Park and it is on your right, before reaching the ticket office. You will find an admirable selection of books on the history and culture of Istanbul

---

❿ *Peacock amidst tulips and carnations: from a 16th-century tiled kiosk*

and Turkey, and CDs of classical folk and contemporary Turkish music. ⓐ Avlusu Sultanahmet, Topkapı Palace ⓣ 0212 513 5082 ⓛ 09.00–17.00 Tues–Sun, closed Mon

İznik Classics Quality ceramics with prices that start at around 15 YTL for small items and go up to 400 YTL. The proprietor has two other shops in the vicinity and you may find yourself being persuaded to make a visit, but there is no compulsion to buy anything. ⓐ Arasta Bazaar 67 ⓣ 0212 517 1705 ⓦ www.iznikclassics ⓛ 08.00–20.30 (summer); 08.30–18.30 (winter)

TAKING A BREAK

Anatolian House £ ❶ A cosy, small eatery off busy Divan Yolu Caddesi that offers welcome relief after a morning's schlepping around the sights. Stuffed aubergines, rice in rolled grape leaves, Turkish ravioli, varied drinks with and without alcohol. ⓐ Divan Yolu Caddesi, Hioca Rüstem Sokak 7 ⓣ 0212 522 0638 ⓛ 08.00–midnight

Caferağa Medresei £ ❷ The perfect resting place for a drink or light lunch after visiting nearby Topkapı Palace is a peaceful courtyard with tables serving meatballs, salad, pastries, coffee or a hot milk with orchid root. While you are here check out the one-day handicraft courses that take place in what used to be the study rooms of an old college and the teachers' work that is for sale. ⓐ Caferiye Sokak ⓣ 0212 513 3601 ⓦ www.tkhv.org ⓛ 08.30–19.00

Konyalı Café £ ❸ The only place to eat inside Topkapı Palace, and if you use the cafeteria service the prices are very reasonable considering the location and the marvellous views of the Sea of

Marmara and the Golden Horn from the terrace or glassed-in pavilion. If you just need a tea or coffee and a *simit* (sesame-topped bread ring), there is a kiosk near the ticket desk for the harem.
ⓐ Topkapı Palace ⓣ 0212 513 9696 ⓛ 10.00–17.00

Sultan Ahmet Köftecisi £ ❹ Justly famous *köfte* (meatball) eatery, established in the 1920s, which has queues forming outside as sunset approaches during Ramadan. Make sure you are eating in the restaurant with the brown façade because other restaurants using the same name have set up in the same street. ⓐ Divan Yolu Caddesi 12 ⓣ 0212 513 1438 ⓦ www.sultanahmetkoftecisi.com/tr

AFTER DARK

Restaurants

Ambassador £ ❺ A neat little rooftop terrace with skyline views of the Blue Mosque and Aya Sofya. A weekly barbecue in the summer, vegetarians catered for and fresh fish from the local market if ordered in advance. Alternatively, come here late just for drinks and the vista. ⓐ Ticarethane Sokak 19 ⓣ 0212 511 9828 ⓦ www.ambassador.com

Café Meşale £ ❻ As it's in the heart of touristy Sultanahmet, few locals eat or drink here, but it is a fun place at night when there is always some live music and singing. You can dine or drink inside or at tables under the night sky in the forecourt area. ⓐ Arasta Bazaar ⓣ 0212 518 9562

Kir Evi ££ ❼ There are many after-dark possibilities in and around this area but Kir Evi wins hands down; cool atmosphere, candlelight, live music at night, friendly service and good-value meals. ⓐ Divan Yolu Caddesi, Hioca Rüstem Sokak 9 ⓣ 0212 512 6942

Magnaura ££ ❽ Funky décor and wooden floors make this a comfortable eatery. The rooftop terrace tables afford wonderful sea views and always get filled up first. ⓐ Akbıyık Caddesi 27 ⓣ 0212 518 7622 ⓦ www.magnauracafereataurant.com

Rami ££ ❾ This Ottoman-style, wood-slatted house, named after the Turkish painter whose works are on display, serves Ottoman dishes in an elegant and romantic setting. As usual, tables on the rooftop terrace need a reservation; it's worth the effort; you will be rewarded with a grand view of the nightly Blue Mosque sound and light show. ⓐ Utangaç Sokak 6 ⓣ 0212 517 6593 ⓦ www.ramiuluer.com

Terrace Marmara ££ ❿ Make a reservation to secure one of the tables with a sublime view of the Blue Mosque. Steaks and kebabs are on offer, but vegetarians can enjoy stuffed aubergine, spinach quiche, and carrot rolls with yoghurt. A cocktail and wine list is also available. ⓐ Blue House (Mavi Ev), Dalbastı Sokak ⓣ 0212 638 9010 ⓦ www.bluehouse.com.tr

ⓐ *Restaurants beckon after dark*

Yesil Ev ££ ⑪ Alfresco dining in a delightful garden setting with
Aya Sofya as the backdrop, or inside a glasshouse with a floral motif.
Kebabs, chicken curry and salads plus hot and cold appetisers.
ⓐ Kabasakal Caddesi 5 ⓣ 0212 517 6785

Sarnic Restaurant £££ ⑫ When the need for the rooftop dining
fling is out of your system it is time to go deep underground and
descend into a cavernous, millennium-old cistern and relish a dark,
candle-lit atmosphere. The food is so-so and the wine list pricey, but
what a location for an evening out. ⓐ Soğuk Çeşme Sokak ⓣ 0212 512
4291 ⓦ www.ayasofyakonaklari.com

Bars, pubs & baths

Çemberlitaş Hamami One of Istanbul's most historic Turkish
baths, dating back to the 16th century. Prices range from 19 YTL
for a bath and a do-it-yourself scrub, to 29 YTL for a bath and
massage or 49 YTL for the full works. ⓐ Vezir Hanı Caddesi 8,
Çemberlitaş ⓣ 0212 522 7974 ⓦ www.cemberlitashamami.com.tr
ⓛ 06.00–24.00

Cheers A popular pub that attracts backpacking budget travellers
from the nearby hostels. There are two more like-minded pubs
a few doors down. ⓐ Akbıyık Caddesi 20 ⓣ 0212 409 6369
ⓛ 10.00–02.00

Sultan Pub An upmarket tourist trap in some respects but the
outdoor tables make for a comfortable pre- or after-dinner
drink; the cocktails are pricey. There is plenty of food of the
pizza-burger-pasta kind. ⓐ Divan Yolu Caddesi 2 ⓣ 0212 511 5638
ⓦ www.sultanpub.com.tr ⓛ 09.30–02.00

Grand Bazaar & surrounds

The Grand Bazaar and its surrounding area is not as compact as Sultanahmet but the tram system serves as a point of reference as well as the means of getting to and from here. It runs past the Grand Bazaar at the Beyazıt stop and continues eastwards, stopping at Sultanahmet and two other stops before reaching Eminönü. At Eminönü there is the Galata Bridge crossing the Golden Horn to Karaköy and the funicular railway that zips you up to the start of İstiklal Caddesi. The sights and attractions of this section, which start at the Grand Bazaar and conclude at Sırkecı railway station near Eminönü, can all be reached on foot, but the tram is a blessing when fatigue sets in.

SIGHTS & ATTRACTIONS

Beyazıt Square

The square is a busy transport junction filled with buses and taxis and the Beyazıt tram stop that is handy for the Grand Bazaar. The military-style building you see to the north of the square is the entrance to Istanbul University but any sense of student life is drowned out by the traffic and crowds of people. Beyazıt Tower, inside the grounds of the university, can be climbed to the top for views over the city. In the square itself stands the grimy Beyazıt Mosque, the oldest surviving mosque in the city, inspired by Aya Sofya and providing a model that would be improved upon with the Süleymaniye Mosque.

Haliç (Golden Horn) & Galata Köprüsü (Galata Bridge)

One of the great sights in Istanbul is the Golden Horn, the never-empty Galata Bridge spanning it, and the constant flow of traffic on

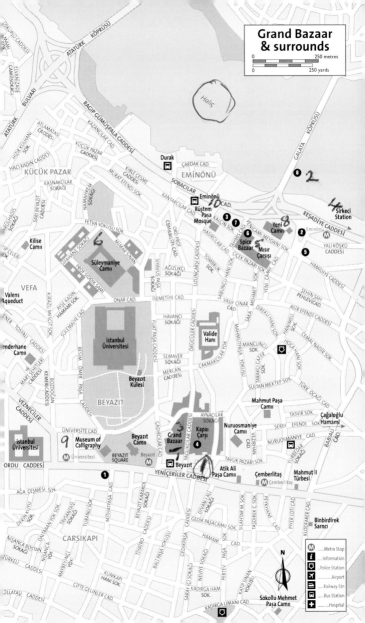

Grand Bazaar & surrounds

0 — 250 metres
0 — 250 yards

Haliç

ATATÜRK KÖPRÜSÜ

ŞİŞKU CADDESİ
EYVAN SOKAĞI
ELVANZADE CAMİSİ SOKAĞI
ATATÜRK BULVARI

RAGIP GÜMÜŞPALA CADDESİ

HACI KADIN CADDESİ
HITIT KÜLHANI SOK
ATLAMATAŞI CADDESİ
KAZANCILAR CAD.
KIBLE ÇEŞME CADDESİ
KÜÇÜK PAZAR CADDESİ
MURAT MOLLA EFENDİ SOK.
SOBACILAR

KÜÇÜK PAZAR

Durak
ÇARDAK CAD.
EMİNÖNÜ

Eminönü
Rüstem Paşa Mosque **10**
KANTARCILAR CAD.
ORO CAD.
CEMBERLİTAŞ
ALICIN SOK.
YENİ CAMİİ MEYDANI SOK.

3 **7**
Yeni Camii **2** Eminönü
5

KASNAKÇILAR SOKAĞI
SAVI BEYAZIT CADDESİ
SABI BEYAZIT SOK.
ZALİF ÇELEBİ

Kilise Camii

VEFA

Valens Aqueduct

FETVA YOKUŞU SOK.
ŞEHZADE SOK.
MİMAR SİNAN

Süleymaniye Camii **6**

PROF. SIDDIK SAMİ
AYŞE KADIN HAMAM SOK.
SÜLEYMANİYE SOK.
KIRAZLI MESCİT SOK.
ŞAIR MEHMET
SIVACI SOK.
AĞIZLIKÇI SOKAĞI
SİVAS PAŞA CAD.
ONAR CAD.
İSMETİYE CAD.
CEMAL NADİR SOK.
HAVANCI SOKAĞI
FUAT PAŞA CADDESİ
SEMAVER SOKAĞI
MERCAN CADDESİ

TENER TOSYALI CAD.
nderhane Camii
MARY ŞEHİTLERİ SOK.
KEMERALTI CAD.
BOZDOĞAN KEMERİ CADDESİ
BESİM ÖMER PAŞA CADDESİ

istanbul Üniversitesi

Beyazıt Külesi

BEYAZIT

VEZNECİLER CADDESİ

istanbul Üniversitesi

ORDU CADDESİ
AĞA ÇEŞMESİ SOK.

ÜNİVERSİTE CAD.

Museum of Calligraphy **9**

Beyazıt Camii
M Üniversitesi
BEYAZIT SQUARE
Beyazıt

YAĞLIKÇILAR CADDESİ
AYNACILAR SOK.

Grand Bazaar **4**
Kapalı Çarşı

TAVUK PAZARI SOK.

Atik Ali Paşa Camii

YENİÇERİLER CADDESİ **1**

CARŞIKAPI

DEVİN KUYU SOK.
TAKKECİLER SOK.
TUBALI SOK.
DALBASAN YOK SOK.
MITHATPAŞA CADDESİ
BEYAZIT KARAKOL SOKAĞI
TİYATRO CADDESİ
BALİ PAŞA YOKUŞU
GEDİK PAŞACAMİİ SOK.
HAMAM
DIVAN ALİ SOK.
NEVŞEHİR SOKAĞI
GEDİKPAŞA CADDESİ

NİŞANCA BOSTAN SOKAĞI
NİŞANCA SOK.
MATBEYINCI YOK.
MAYBEYİNCİ YOK.
ŞEKERCİ CAD.
KUMKAPI HANI SOK.
SARAY İÇİ SOKAĞI
KADİRGA HAM. SOK.
KATİP SİNAN YOKUŞU
KADİRGA LİMANI CAD.
ÇİFTE GELİNLER CAD.
OLLATAŞI CADDESİ

Sokollu Mehmet Paşa Camii

SEHİN ŞAH PEHLEVİ CAD.
HAMİDİYE CADDESİ
RESADİYE CADDESİ
Sirkeci Station
GALATA KÖPRÜSÜ
YALI KÖŞKÜ CADDESİ **5**
8 **2**

Misir Çarşısı
Spice Bazaar **6**
ÇİÇEK PAZARI SOK.
HASIRCILAR CAD.
UZUNÇARŞI CADDESİ
TOMRUK SOK.
SABUNCU HANI SOK.
VASIF ÇINAR CAD.
DİREKLİ HAN SOK.
YENİ CAMİİ CADDESİ
ASİR EFENDİ CADDESİ

Valide Hanı
ORUCULER CADDESİ
ÇAKMAKÇILAR YOKUŞU
MAHMUTPAŞA YOKUŞU
MANCUNCU SOK.
HANIMELİ SOK.
HOCA HAN SOK.
TARAKÇI CAFER SOK.
SULTAN MEKTEP SOK.
TÜRK OCAĞI CAD.

Mahmut Paşa Camii
TASVİR SOK.
ŞERİF EFENDİ SOK.
NURUOSMANİYE CADDESİ
TÜRBEDAR SOKAĞI
BABIALİ CADDESİ

Çağaloğlu Hamamı

Nuruosmaniye Camii **M** Çemberlitaş
Çemberlitaş
Mahmut II Türbesi

DİVAN ALİ SOK.
SİLAHTAR M. SOK.
TAŞDİRE. C. SOK.
FEVZİ PAŞA SOK.
PİYER LOTİ CAD.
KLODFARER CAD.

Binbirdirek Sarnıcı

N

M Metro Stop
i Information
∅ Police Station
✈ Airport
⊟ Railway Stn
⊟ Bus Station
✚ Hospital

the water. The ancient Greeks spotted its potential in the 7th century BC and it has been growing in importance ever since. It has also grown richer if you believe the story behind the name; the Byzantines threw so many riches into it when the Ottomans attacked that the surface sparkled with gold. It still sparkles at night with the twinkling lights of boats and ferries and walking across it at dusk and pausing in the middle to take in the whole scene offers a stirring sight of the great city. The bridge is underslung with fish restaurants and on a summer's evening it pays to linger here if only for a drink or two.

Grand Bazaar

It is hard to say whether you will like or loathe the Grand Bazaar. To some it is full of character and imbued with an ambience wherein you can lose yourself, literally and figuratively; to others the place is a claustrophobic den where predatory merchants appear out of nowhere and where nothing can be bought without endless haggling. It probably depends on your mood, but see it you should; it is a fascinating, veritable labyrinth of streets with some 4,000 shops, including restaurants and cafés. Avoid Saturday, when it becomes just too crowded to enjoy. There are signposts at various junctions within the bazaar but you will have a hard job retracing your exact route and the chances are you will exit at a different point from your entrance.

ⓐ Kapali Carsi ⏱ 08.30–19.00, closed Sun

Sirkeci Station

The traffic here is busy and distracting, but stroll around the station a couple of times to take in the details, and its architectural merits begin to be noticed. Functionality combines with Byzantine and

Ottoman stylistic features and inside there is a splendidly old-fashioned restaurant, an impressive waiting room and a small museum devoted to the Orient Express. There is also a tourist office.

🔺 *Spice up your trip at the Spice Bazaar*

Spice Bazaar

It is a matter of temperament, perhaps, if you prefer the Spice Bazaar to the Grand Bazaar, but if you want your senses played on in a minor but exquisite key then this is the market to visit. Built in the late 17th century, it still evokes the Ottoman world even though the shops selling spices, the special merchandise of this bazaar brought up along the Golden Horn from all quarters of the Ottoman Middle East, are now matched in number by those bulging with souvenirs, handicrafts and dubious aphrodisiacs. There is a famous restaurant on the premises (see page 86) if you feel the need for a break but, unlike the Grand Bazaar, the Spice Bazaar is not big or crowded enough to drain all your energy. The Spice Bazaar's name, by the way, comes from the fact that it was built from import duties levied on goods from Egypt.

ⓐ Eminönü ⓛ 08.30–18.30 Mon–Sat, closed Sun

Süleymaniye Camıı (Süleymaniye Mosque)

Mimar Sinan, the best of the Ottoman architects, designed this mosque complex for Süleyman the Magnificent and what a superb

THE ORIENT EXPRESS

On its maiden run in 1889 the Orient Express chugged out of Paris and steamed 2,900 km (1,800 miles) in three days before pulling into its Istanbul destination at Sirkeci Station. The station and the Pera Palas Hotel (see page 90) were built for the Orient Express and both places continue to evoke that bygone era – with the help of Agatha Christie's *Murder on the Orient Express*, Graham Greene's *Stamboul Express*, and half a dozen films. The last train from Paris pulled into Istanbul in 1977.

building it still is. The unadorned interior is stunning and the sense of equilibrium created by the open space is founded on geometry: the height of the dome is precisely double its diameter. In the adjoining cemetery you can admire the impressive tomb of Süleyman that shines with inlaid ceramic stars. Here, too, is the tomb of his all-powerful wife Roxelana.

ⓐ Prof Sıddık Onar Caddesi ☏ 0212 514 0139

🕐 09.30–17.30 (but avoid visiting during Friday prayers); donation requested

Valens Aqueduct

Named after the Roman emperor who had the aqueduct built in the 4th century to bring water into the city, it functioned as such well into the 19th century. Now it straddles a busy road and is distant from other attractions, but if you take the Havaş airport bus to or from Taksim Square, you will pass underneath the structure and get a good impression of its mighty size.

ⓐ Atatürk Bulvari

Yeni Camıı (New Mosque)

It is impossible to miss seeing this monumental mosque because it dominates the Eminönü neighbourhood and the view coming over the Galata Bridge from the other side of the Golden Horn. Completed in the mid-17th century and the last of the great Ottoman mosques, its exterior is its most prepossessing feature and you are likely to be disappointed by the relatively dull interior. The plaza outside has some seats and low stone walls where you can picnic (with the pigeons) on a fine day.

ⓐ Yenicami Meydanı Sokak, Eminönü ☏ 0212 527 8505 🕐 09.30–17.30 (but avoid visiting during Friday prayers)

MIMAR SINAN

The great architect Mimar Sinan (circa 1491–1588) came from Anatolia but his talents were spotted at a young age and he was brought to study in Istanbul. He was working as an engineer when Süleyman the Magnificent promoted him to chief architect and the sultan was rewarded with plans for the Süleymaniye Mosque and Rüstem Paşa Mosque. These are certainly Mimar Sinan's finest achievements, but he designed well over a hundred mosques and many other buildings, including the Çemberlitaş baths.

CULTURE

Museum of Calligraphy

On the west side of Beyazıt Square this small museum will reward your time only if you are predisposed to appreciating the fine art of Ottoman calligraphy. The meaning of the words will mean nothing but the skilled precision of the calligrapher, akin to the achievement of the monks who inscribed the *Book of Kells*, takes on its own beauty. Some of the calligrapher's tools are also on display here, plus miniatures from the Ottoman period.

ⓐ Türk Vakıf Hat Sanatları Müzesi, Beyazıt Square ⓣ 0212 527 5851
ⓒ 09.00–16.00 Tues–Sat, closed Sun; admission charge

Rüstem Paşa Mosque

Within easy walking distance of the Spice Bazaar, this delightful, mid-16th-century mosque does not impose itself physically – it is easy to miss altogether – and it is only when you are inside that its

ⓞ *One of Yeni Camıı's aspiring minarets*

cultural richness makes an impression. The quality of the İznik tiles is unrivalled, especially on the galleries, and there are beautiful patterns and pictorial panels to admire, all clearly lit with the natural light flowing in through the multitude of windows.
ⓐ Hasırcılar Caddesi ☏ 0212 526 7350 ⏰ 08.30–16.30 (but avoid visiting during Friday prayers)

RETAIL THERAPY

Ali Muhiddin Hacı Bekir If you get off the tram at Sirkeci Railway Station, Hamidiye Caddesi is almost directly in front of you and down here on the left, opposite Hafiz Mustafa Şekerlemeleri (see page 85) is a very historic shop, claiming to be the first place in the city to sell *lokum* (Turkish delight). This is not tourist hype, as shown by the Turkish customers waiting to purchase one of the many varieties on sale, including plain, hazelnut and pistachio.
ⓐ Hamidiye Caddesi 83, Eminönü ☏ 0212 522 0666 ⏰ 08.00–20.00 Mon–Sat, 09.00–20.00 Sun

GNHN47 Three floors of fabrics and a modest selection of jewellery in the heart of the Spice Bazaar. The prices of the pretty shawls vary according to the quality of the embroidery and some bargaining will be the order of the day. If engaged in small-talk with sellers, try asking them what the name of the shop signifies.
ⓐ Mısır Caddesi 47, Spice Bazaar ☏ 0212 522 3840 ⏰ 08.00–19.00, closed Sun

M and K You will pass this shop on your left if approaching the Grand Bazaar along Tavukpazarı from the Çemberlitaş tram stop. Pop in for Iranian caviar (US$5 a gram), candyfloss, Turkish olive oil in

tins, Turkish chocolate, or Turkish packed honeycomb.
🅐 Tavukpazarı 37 🕿 0212 520 7063 🕒 09.00–19.00, closed Sun

Muhliş Günbatti A specialist shop for *suzani* (hand-appliquéd
fabric) from Turkey's eastern neighbours, Turkmenistan and
Uzbekistan, and a choice selection of Ottoman kaftans and kilims.
🅐 Perçacilar Sokak 48, Grand Bazaar 🕿 0212 511 6562 🕒 09.00–17.00,
closed Sun

Özer A handicraft shop in the Spice Bazaar, Özer retails embroidered
silk, cotton, cashmere and jewellery, and downstairs there are
decorative home textiles. An attractive store and no hard sell.
🅐 Mısır Caddesi 82, Spice Bazaar 🕿 0212 526 8079 🕢 www.ozer.org
🕒 09.30–18.30, closed Sun

Şişko Osman This is a well-established carpet store in the
Grand Bazaar and the carpets, rugs and kilims are quality items.
There is another outlet of the same company in the Grand
Bazaar, with the same name, in Zincirli Han Caddesi. 🅐 Halıcılar
Caddesi 49, Grand Bazaar 🕿 0212 526 1708 🕒 09.00–18.00,
closed Sun

TAKING A BREAK

Beyazıt Internet Café £ ❶ Facing Istanbul University to the north
in Beyazıt Square, look behind you and the sign for this café is hard
to miss. Tea, coffee and confectionery are for sale and pleasant
window seats overlook the busy scene down on the street. Chess
boards are also at hand. 🅐 Yeniçeriler Caddesi, Uluçay İşhanı 47,
Beyazıt Square 🕿 0212 638 8337 🕒 09.00–24.00

APHRODISIAQUE DES SULTANS
MESIR MACUNU

FIYATLARIMIZA
KDV
DAHILDIR.

Borsa £ ❷ Crossing Yalıköşkü Caddesi from the Golden Horn side by the pedestrian bridge, Borsa is tucked away behind the bottom of the steps. A lovely clean and modern *lokanta* (traditional Turkish restaurant), with a self-service counter, and an excellent choice of traditional Turkish dishes. Raki and cappuccino also available.
📍 Yalıköşkü Caddesi 60, Eminönü 📞 0212 511 8079 🕐 09.00–20.00

Coffee World £ ❸ Standing in the open square next to the New Mosque, with the Golden Horn behind you, this pleasant alfresco café is in the top right corner of the square. Shaded from the heat and providing a restful spot after a visit to the Spice Bazaar, it offers a choice of good coffee and light snacks. 📍 Off Tahmis Caddesi, Eminönü 📞 0212 520 0204 🕐 08.00–16.00

Fez Café £ ❹ This is one of the best-known cafés inside the Grand Bazaar and its boho décor (check the Philippe Starck-designed chairs) blends in perfectly with the location. If there are no vacant tables for the sage tea and carrot cake, the Sultan Café next door is just as good, or pop around the corner to the neon-lit Divan Café Pastcinesi for cakes and cream with lower prices than the Fez.
📍 Halıcılar Caddesi 62, Grand Bazaar 📞 0212 527 3684
🕐 08.30–1900, closed Sun

Hafiz Mustafa Şekerlemeleri £ ❺ This is a busy part of town and, if you have just walked over the Galata Bridge, finding somewhere quiet for a cup of tea and a snack is not easy. Hafiz Mustafa Şekerlemeleri looks like a cake and *lokum* (Turkish delight) deli, but climb the stairs at the back and you'll find a small eating area, having ordered your drinks

◀ *Love potions and loofas at the Spice Bazaar*

and cakes downstairs. ⓐ Hamidiye Caddesi 86, Eminönü ⓣ 0212 526
5627 ⓛ 08.00–20.00 Mon–Sat, 09.00–20.00 Sun

Pandeli ££ ⓺ Just inside the Spice Bazaar, this is a very well-known
restaurant, artfully decorated with İznik tiles and benefiting from an
air of faded elegance. Not a cheap lunch, but the aubergine dishes
are good. A reservation is advisable. ⓐ Mısır Caddesi 82, Spice Bazaar
ⓣ 0212 522 5534 ⓛ 09.00–15.30, closed Sun

AFTER DARK

Restaurants
Hamdi £ ⓻ Come here after dark to relish the atmospheric views
over the Golden Horn and enjoy Turkish kebabs at their best – and
not just plain old kebabs, but pistachio or aubergine ones, with
yoghurt or garlic. Really rather good. Find the stairs through the
ground-floor eatery. ⓐ Tahmis Caddesi, Kalçın Sokak 17, Eminönü
ⓣ 0212 528 0390 ⓦ www.hamdirestaurant.com ⓛ 10.00–23.00

Yagalata ££ ⓼ Under Galata Bridge you are spoilt for choice when
it comes to fish restaurants and at Yagalata you also have to choose
from a variety of fish: bonito, lobster, swordfish, natural and farmed
sea bass, and turbot. Sit outside and maximise the unique location,
or stay inside for the air conditioning and more comfort. ⓐ Galata
Bridge, Eminönü ⓣ 0212 514 4777 ⓦ www.onnumaracafe.com
ⓛ 11.00–24.00

Baths & concerts
Cağaloğlu Hamamı A beautifully baroque, 18th-century *hamam*
and, yes, it has been used in film sets (one of the Indiana Jones

escapades). As with Çemberlitaş Hamami (see page 73) there is a choice of treatments from the basic DIY job to the luxury massage.

ⓐ Prof. Kazım Ismail Caddesi, Cağaloğlu ⓣ 0212 522 2424
ⓛ 08.00–22.00 (men); 08.00–21.00 (women)

Turkish Mystic Music & Dance This Sufi music concert and whirling dervishes ceremony is performed by a group from the Galata Mevlevihanesi (see page 91) in the characterful setting of a hall by platform 1 of the famous Sirkeci Railway Station. The railway restaurant is handily close for a drink before or after the show.

ⓐ Sirkeci Railway Station ⓣ 0212 458 8834 ⓛ 19.30 Sun, Wed & Fri; admission charge

△ There are many attractive squares for diners around the Grand Bazaar

Karaköy to Galatasaray

The sights in this area are listed in the order you will encounter them if walking across the Galata Bridge from Eminönü into the old port area of Karaköy, then to Galata where the Tünel funicular railway whisks you up to İstiklal Caddesi, and halfway up the pedestrianised street, as far as Galatasaray. This whole area on the other side of the Golden Horn used to be called Pera and is rich in attractions, both ancient and modern, and everywhere can be reached on foot.

PERA

Pera, from the Greek for 'across' or 'beyond', became shorthand for the other side of the Golden Horn from Constantinople, now the areas of Galata and Beyoğlu. In time, and when Istanbul was the capital of Turkey, it became the European quarter of the city and foreign embassies (now just consulates) were established here, hence the tales of intrigue and spying that could give a dangerous edge to expatriate life in old Stamboul. At the same time, it became the shopping ground for affluent Europeans off the Orient Express.

SIGHTS & ATTRACTIONS

Church of SS Peter and Paul

The Dominican Brothers saw their own church converted to a mosque so they moved to this location and established a new base. The church you see today was built in the mid-19th century and is entered through a courtyard – Ottoman regulations would not

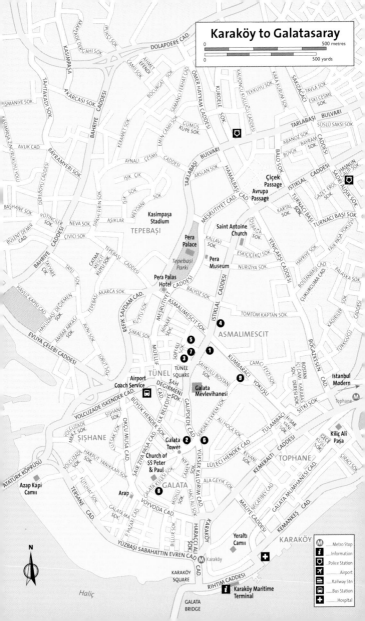

allow a church façade to face the street directly – and you may have to search to find the doorway.
ⓐ Galata Kulesi Sokak 44 ⓣ 0212 245 1160 ⓛ 09.00–19.00

Galata Tower

Built by the Genoans in 1348 and used as a watchtower, Galata Tower has been restored a number of times and is now a solid structure boasting some of the finest views of the city on a fine day. The restaurant and evening show that take place at the top are, frankly, forgettable, but a drink can be enjoyed while taking in the vista.
ⓐ Galata Kulesi, Karaköy ⓣ 0212 293 8180 ⓦ www.galatatower.net
ⓛ 09.00–20.00; admission charge

Pera Palas Hotel

You can stay at this expensive institution (see page 38) or just wander in for refreshments in the *fin-de-siècle* patisserie or bar and soak up the atmosphere of this wonderfully unique hotel. Where other great hotels of the past, like the Raffles in Singapore, have been manicured beyond recognition, the Pera Palas is virtually unchanged since it opened in 1892. There is a roll-call of famous guests, including Trotsky, Greta Garbo and Jackie Chan, on the wall near the antique lift, and in the bar there is a display cabinet relating a curious mystery about a key found in room 411 where Agatha Christie stayed.
ⓐ Meşrutiyet Caddesi 98, Tepebaşı ⓣ 0212 251 4560

Avrupa Pasaji (Avrupa Passage)

Evocative of bourgeois Pera, the handsome but narrow, glass-roofed, marble-floored arcades that grace Istanbul can be walked past without being noticed. They are gems of urban architecture, modelled on Parisian arcades, and this one is filled with character.

🅐 Avrupa Pasajı, off Sahne Sokak

Çiçek Pasaji (Cicek Passage)

Another gorgeous arcade, this one is in the old Cité de Pera building that was once an almost obligatory stop for the rich and fashionable arriving in the city. Built in the 1870s, it fell into disrepair but has been renovated and polished up rather nicely. There is a popular eating complex at the back, and the adjoining fish market is certainly worth a quick look.

CULTURE

Galata Mevlevihanesi

This centre of Sufi culture, originally a monastery and now a small museum, is the venue for ceremonies of the famous whirling dervishes, the Mevlevis, most Sundays at 15.00 (phone in advance to

---

THE WHIRLING DERVISHES

Adherents of Sufism, a mystical branch of Islam, aspire to personal and ecstatic contact with the divine through dance, music and recitation. The best known of the various sects of Sufism are the Mevlevi, known as the Whirling Dervishes because of their fast, spinning dance, the *sema*, that aims for a trance-like communion with the spiritual realm of existence. The first dervishes were followers of the 13th-century Sufi guru Jelaleddn Rumi and the dancers who perform today are devotees of the sect.

make sure). Sufism was banned by the reforming Atatürk in the 1920s and this monastery survived only by turning itself into an educational institution.

ⓐ Galipedede Caddesi 15 ⓣ 0212 245 4141 ⓛ 09.30–17.00, closed Mon

Istanbul Modern

This is contemporary Istanbul – artistic and dynamic – alive to the international arts scene but keen to make art accessible to all. A permanent exhibition of modern Turkish art, a large space for retrospectives and international exhibitions and a photography gallery are all here. The entrance area showcases trends in video and interactive works of art.

ⓐ Meclis-i-Mebusan Caddesi, Liman İşletmeleri Sahası Atrepo 4, Karaköy ⓣ 0212 334 7300 ⓦ www.istanbulmodern.org
ⓛ 10.00–18.00, closed Mon; admission charge but free on Thur 10.00–14.00

Pera Museum

The Istanbul Modern could have been a one-off but the opening of the Pera Museum in 2005 confirmed Istanbul's status as the cultural capital of Turkey. The building itself is architecturally beautiful, built in the late 19th century but meticulously renovated to house four floors of exhibition space. Two levels are devoted to a permanent exhibition of Anatolian weights and measures and a collection of tiles and ceramics, but what may grab your attention are the international exhibitions (Henri Cartier-Bresson, for example) that the museum's private funds are capable of mounting.

ⓐ Meşrutiyet Caddesi 141, Tepebası ⓣ 0212 334 9900
ⓦ www.peraartgallery.com ⓛ 10.00–19.00 Tues–Sat, 12.00–18.00 Sun, closed Mon; free admission

RETAIL THERAPY

Art Ena Down a side-street, on your left off Galata Kulesi Sokak (which leads to Nardis Jazz Club and Galata House (see pages 99 and 97)), this little shop and café retails jewellery, accessories and home-made tops and scarves. Try the gear on and then tuck into cheesecake, chocolate, sandwiches and coffee. ⓐ Camekan Sokak 1 ⓘ 0212 292 3383 ⓒ 09.00–21.00

◐ *Almost unchanged since 1892 – the patisserie at the Pera Palas Hotel*

Artrium Turkish miniatures, calligraphy, paintings, cards, prints, movie posters, ceramics, and custom jewellery all mixed together; you'll feel as if you may unearth something priceless among all the stock. ❸ Tünel Geçidi 7 ❶ 0212 251 4302 ◔ 09.00–19.00, closed Sun

Beyoğlu Hali Evi Affordable hand-painted ceramics – plates, bowls, tea- and coffee-sets – and a reasonable choice. ❸ İstiklal Caddesi 388, Tünel ❶ 0212 293 9990 ◔ 09.00–20.00

Golden Sound On your right if walking down Kumbaracı Yokuşu towards Leb-i Derya (see page 97), the musical instruments for sale here are handmade on the premises. ❸ Kumbaracı Yokuşu ❶ 0212 293 6659 ◔ 09.30–21.00

Robinson Crusoe One of the best bookshops in the city for English-language publications, including books about Istanbul and Turkey and a good range of current magazines. ❸ İstiklal Caddesi 389 ❶ 0212 293 6968 ◔ 09.00–21.30, closed Sun

Sedef Gür One-off designs and specialist clothing and accessories. ❸ Çukurcuma Caddesi 74, Beyoğlu ❶ 0212 249 0896

TAKING A BREAK

Armada £ ❶ A useful restaurant for an inexpensive lunch on İstiklal Caddesi in a bright and clean eatery offering kebabs, *köfte* (meatballs) and other Turkish favourites. ❸ İstiklal Caddesi 467 ❶ 0212 249 7927 ◔ 09.00–21.30

Güney Restaurant £ ❷ If you forsake the funicular and leg it up to Galata from the bridge, you will need some refreshment and this old favourite does the business. No alcohol, but coffees and kebabs, *mezes* (Turkish starters) and chicken dishes. ⓐ Kuledibi Şahkapısı Sokak 6 ❶ 0212 249 0393 ❶ 07.30–22.00, closed Sun

⬤ *An architectural treasure on the street*

KeVe £–££ ❸ Step out of the funicular railway at Tünel and this arcaded courtyard is immediately opposite. It tends to attract the self-conscious arty types with time on their hands, but retains its appeal as a calm and green oasis for tea, coffee or something stronger accompanying carrot cake or maybe figs marinated in cognac. ⓐ Tünel Square 10 ❶ 0212 251 4338 ⓦ www.kc.com.tr ❶ 08.30–02.00

Sushico £–££ ❹ Japanese and Thai in a modern, fresh setting and at reasonable prices. Six sushi rolls for anything from 5 YTL (egg) to 20 YTL (caviar), tasty vegetable tempura and set good-value meals. ⓐ İstiklal Caddesi 445, Tünel ❶ 0212 243 8765 ⓦ www.sushico.com.tr ❶ 12.00–23.00

AFTER DARK

Restaurants
Refik £ ❺ Refik has been around for some time and benefits from a good reputation as an informal restaurant where good Turkish

ARTY EATING
The über-smart restaurant at the Istanbul Modern (see page 92) is the ideal place for a drink and/or meal, not so much for the food but for a table by the large plate-glass window overlooking the sea. The chances are that a merchant vessel will be berthed just yards away behind the glass. Alternatively, there is a complex of less expensive eateries on your right as you approach the gallery after turning into it from Necatibey Caddesi.

food and reasonable priced wine can be enjoyed. ❸ Sofyali Sokak 7
❶ 0212 245 7879 ❷ 11.30–24.00 Mon–Sat, 18.30–23.30 Sun

Venta Del Toro £ ❻ Spanish cuisine in this airy and cheerful
restaurant takes the form of tapas, toasted peppers, aubergine and
goat's cheese, and quiche calamari, to name a few items. Turkish
dishes and wines are on offer but Spanish wines also feature on the
expansive drinks list. Live music on Wed, Fri and Sat. ❸ Galipdede
Caddesi 145, Galata ❶ 0212 243 6049

Lokal £–££ ❼ This little eatery (no more than 20 people can be
seated at any one time) is typical of the creative flair that makes this
end of Beyoğlu such an exciting place on the contemporary food
scene. The menu is hard to pin down but there is a definite Thai edge
to what is on offer. ❸ Müeyyet Sokak 9, off İstiklal Caddesi ❶ 0212 245
5743 ❷ 10.30–23.00 Mon–Thur, 10.30–01.30 Fri & Sat, 10.30–22.00 Sun

Galata House ££ ❽ Western powers at one stage had their own
jurisdiction over their citizens' misdemeanours and this building
was the British prison between 1904 and 1919. Complete with
original cell door and prisoners' graffiti, this charming restaurant
has tables in what was the tiny exercise yard, and live music at
night. Indoor dining during the winter. ❸ Galata Kulesi Sokak 61
❶ 0212 245 1861 ❿ www.thegalatahouse.com

Leb-i Derya ££ ❾ Outstanding, wood-and-glass rooftop venue for
after-dark drinks or a meal; take the lift up to the fifth level. Popular
and therefore busy, consider coming also for brunch. Ottoman-style
food and cool views. ❸ Kumbaracı Yokuşu 115, off İstiklal Caddesi
❶ 0212 293 4989 ❷ 09.00–02.00

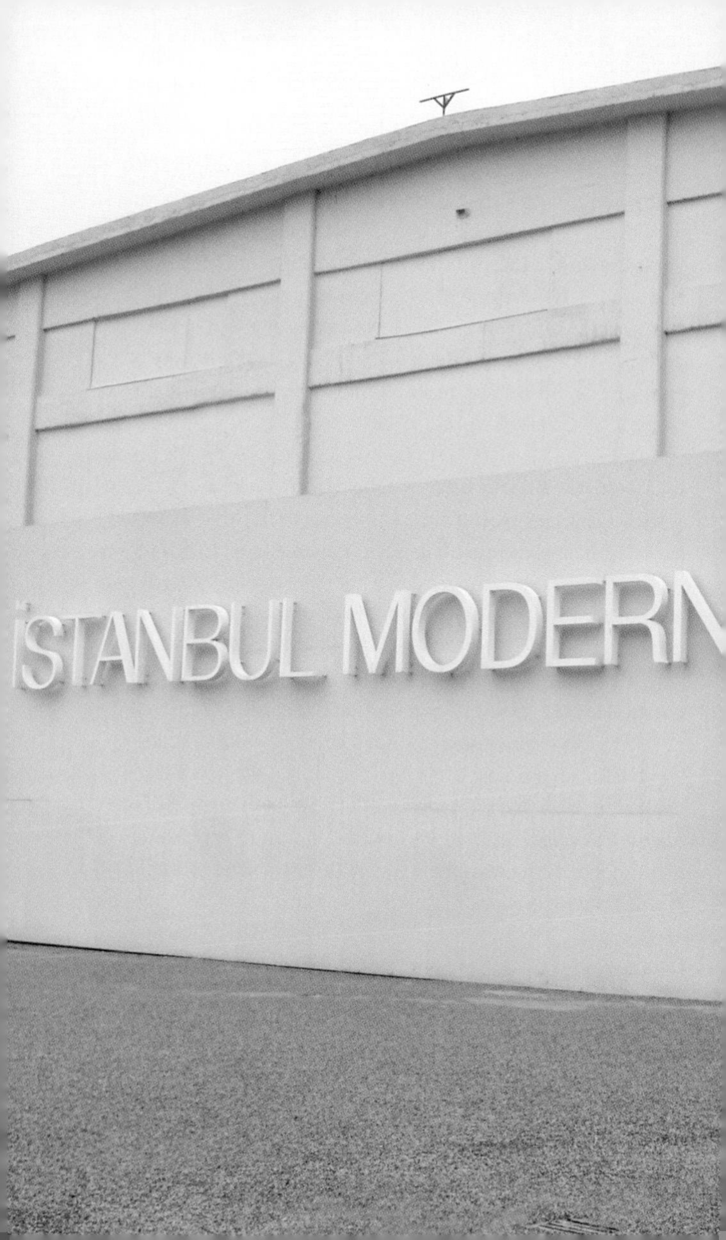
İSTANBUL MODERN

Bars & clubs

Babylon Premier live music club with the programme changing monthly and, every month, an Oldies but Goldies night for nostalgia-ravers. Book in advance for big events. Directly opposite the nightclub is a cosy little joint, appropriately named Little Wing, serving vegetarian food and Turkish herbal teas. A lot less expensive than the drinks in Babylon and open until 01.00. ❷ Seybender Sokak 3, Tünel ❶ 0212 292 7368 ❿ www.babylon-ist.com ❶ 21.30–02.00

Nardis Jazz Club Live performances nightly in the city's best jazz club, named after a Miles Davis song. Ethnic, fusion, modern or classical – take what comes – and food too. ❷ Galata Kulesi Sokak 14 ❶ 0212 244 6327 ❿ www.nardisjazz.com ❶ 22.00–01.00 Mon–Thur, 23.00–02.00 Fri & Sat; cover charge

Sokak Kahvesi A neat and unpretentious watering hole for a raki or two early in the evening and a safe port of call for a late-night drink. Cool music through the speakers and a useful notice board for current entertainment events. ❷ Asmalı Mescit Sokak 13, off İstiklal Caddesi ❶ 0212 251 9396 ❶ 11.00–24.00

◐ *A converted warehouse, setting the art agenda for Istanbul*

Taksim Square & beyond

This area takes in the continuation of İstiklal Caddesi as far as
Taksim Square, from where the T4 bus from Sultanahmet arrives
and departs. Many of the bars and restaurants are tucked away in
side-streets off İstiklâl Caddesi and around Taksim Square and can
be easily reached on foot. The sights and cultural attractions are
more spread out and buses and taxis are often needed to avoid
lengthy walks. The 40T bus service is a useful one, accessing
Ortaköy and Beşiktaş. Dolmabahçe Palace and the Bosphorus
waterfront can be reached on foot from Taksim Square but
the road network is designed for vehicles and pedestrians are
relegated to an inferior status. Returning from Ortaköy in
the early hours of the morning is best done by taxi, though
you will be paying the increased night rate.

SIGHTS & ATTRACTIONS

Boho Galatasaray

This area of Beyoğlu, and the smaller neighbourhood of
Çukurcuma within it (called the 'Soho of Istanbul') that lies
between Sıraselviler Caddesi and İstiklal Caddesi, is a charming
maze of quiet backstreets best taken in by way of an unhurried
stroll (see page 44). It has become a cosmopolitan centre for
small shops and mini design emporiums where you rummage
delicately for authentic Ottoman fabrics and antiques (see 'Retail
therapy' on page 107) and there are restaurants to check out
along the way and maybe return to at night. It's an easy walk
here from Taksim Square.

Taksim Square & beyond

N

0   200 metres
0   200 yards

Key
- Ⓜ Metro Stop
- ⓘ Information
- Police Station
- ✈ Airport
- 🚉 Railway Stn
- 🚌 Bus Station
- ✚ Hospital

BEYBOSTANI SOK

ÇEVRE OTO YOLU

KUZGUNCUK

BOZACI SOK

BABA NAKKAŞ SOK

ÇIFTE ÇINAR SOKAK

CADIYE CADDESI

KUZGUNCUK ÇARŞI CADDESI

HACI BAKKAL SOKAK

YAZMACI SOKAK

BLANCENOS CAD

CUMHURIYET CAD

PAŞALIMANI

PAŞALIMANI CADDESI

ÜSKÜDAR

ÇEVRE OTO YOLU

BOSPHORUS KÖPRÜSÜ

ORTAKÖY

MULLIM NAC CAD

KIRECKEE SOKAK

✚

8

3

5

ORTAKÖY DEREBOYU CADDESI

ÇEVIRMECI SOKAK

ÇIRAĞAN CADDESI

9

PALANGA CADDESI

Şale Köşkü

Yıldız Parkı

YILDIZ

Çırağan Sarayı

BEŞIKTAŞ

MUZEYYEZ CADDESI

Bosphorus

BARBAROS BULVARI

ÇELENIK SOK

REFIK ŞEVKETBEY YOK

MUSTAFA İZZET EFENDI SOKAK

BARBAROS BULVARI

YILDIZ POSTA CADDESI

UZUNÇOVA SOK

İHLAMUR DEREŞI CADDESI

İhlamur Kasrı

EMİRHAN CADDESI

HAKKI TEFEN CADDESI

NÜZHETIYE CADDESI

İHLAMUR CADDESI

MAÇKA

DILMEN SOK

ŞAIR NEDIM CADDESI

ⓘ

Deniz Müzesi

DOLMABAHÇE CADDESI

Dolmabahçe Palace

TEŞVİKIYE

SIRTUSTU SOKAK

HÜSNÜ GEREDE CAD

Teknik Okul

Maçka Parkı

SPOR CAD

BAYILDIM CAD

Swissotel

7

Saat Kulesi

Dolmabahçe Mosque

Kabataş Ferry & Sea Bus Deck

MAÇKA CAD

10

VALI KONAĞI CADDESI

HAKKI TEFEN CADDESI

Askeri Müzesi

KADIRGALAR CADDESI

İnönü Stadium

MECLİSİ MEBUSAN CADDESI

İstanbul Modern

✚

ASKARGAZI

KUMELI CADDESI

ABIDE-I HÜRRIYET CAD

VALI KONAĞI CADDESI

CADDESI

DOLAPDERE CADDESI

HARBIYE

BABIL SOK

KURTULUŞ SOK

EMLAK CAD

Divan Hotel

Havaş Airport Bus Stop

TAKSIM CADDESI

Atatürk Cultural Centrum

MTE CADDESI

TAKSIM

Taksim Square

CUMHURIYET CADDESI

İNÖNÜ CADDESI

The Marmara

2

4

1

6

KABATAŞ

MERİSAN CAD

✚

BOHO

NECATIBEY CADDESI

GALATASARAY

YENIÇARŞI CADDESI

AKSU YOK

SAKIZAĞACI CAD

TARLABAŞI BULVARI

İSTIKLAL CADDESI

FERIKÖY CADDESI

KUTUBAŞI SOK

AKARCA CADDESI

EVRANOŞZADE

GEDIZ SOK

FELEK SOK

EŞREF SAATI CAD

BOZKURT CADDESI

KURTULUŞ CADDESI

TURGUT ÖZ CAD

Çırağan Sarayı (Çırağan Palace)

Çırağan Palace was built as a comfort zone and sumptuous pad for Sultan Abdulmecid, but by the time it was completed in 1874, another sultan was on the throne and he was either murdered or committed suicide inside the palace. At one stage it also housed the Turkish parliament, until it was accidentally burned down in 1910. Now it has been restored to its former glory and function and is once again providing luxury accommodation, though this time to anyone splashing out at the Çırağan Palace Kempinski Hotel (see page 113 for a night out at its Tügra restaurant). Even if you opted not to blow your holiday budget on a room in the palace, you're free to wander in and have a look around.

ⓐ Çırağan Caddesi 84 ❶ 0212 258 3377 ⓦ www.cirigan-palace.com
Ⓝ Bus: T4 from Sultanahmet, then a ten-minute walk, or 40T from Taksim Square

Ihlamur Kasrı (Pavilion of the Linden Tree)

The Pavilion of the Linden Tree, another one-time residence of pleasure-seeking sultans, is as pleasant as the name suggests; a green oasis complete with fountains and flowering magnolias in summer, but no trace of the linden (lime) trees that must have been here at one time. There are two pavilions, designed by the architect of Dolmabahçe Palace – and it shows, so if you enjoyed the palace and wish to see more of the same, the Ihlamur Kasrı is worth a visit. There is a café occupying one of the pavilions and the main one is visited by way of a guided tour.

ⓐ Ihlamer-Teşvikiye Yolu, Beşiktaş ❶ 0212 259 5086 ❷ 09.30–17.00 Tues–Sun, closed Mon (summer); 09.00–15.00 Tues–Sun, closed Mon (winter); admission charge Ⓝ Bus: 40T

Ⓞ *A merry-go-round of vehicles at the heart of modern Istanbul*

Ortaköy

Once a fishing village separated from the city, Ortaköy is now the most fashionable part of the long strip of outdoor bars, clubs and restaurants that stretches from Beşiktaş near Dolmabahçe Palace. It jumps into high gear between April and autumn and at weekends attracts a high-octane crowd of Turkish revellers and jet-setters. It is theatrical and exuberant, perhaps a little too brash for its own good, but it serves as a dynamic reminder that there is more to Istanbul than Byzantine remains and ancient buildings. The quayside square is the epicentre of social life and here on the waterfront, amid all the razzmatazz, sits the solemn and stately Mecidiye Mosque, built in 1855 by the architect of Dolmabahçe Palace.

🚍 Bus: 40T

Taksim Square

The square is certainly not the prettiest sight in Istanbul, being a transport hub with forlorn patches of green struggling to survive, but this is the heart of modern Istanbul. Two buildings dominate – the Marmara Hotel (see page 38) and the Atatürk Cultural Centre – while the monument at the western side features Atatürk and fellow leaders of the Turkish Republic. As well as the bus service to and from Sultanahmet, the Havaş airport bus arrives and departs from Cumhuriyet Caddesi that runs north from the square.

Yıldız Parkı

A spacious green area punctuated with pavilions, small museums, villas and lakes, this park is ideal for a picnic. Much of what you see was put together under Sultan Abdul Hamit II in the late 19th century and he chose to live here much of the time because he was worried that Dolmabahçe Palace might be attacked from the

Bosphorus. The cultural highlight, and the most impressive building in the park, is the Şale Köşkü (Sale Pavilion, see page 107). There are places to drink and eat in the park but if you fancy some heavy-duty pampering in an opulent setting, then it is only a short walk to the Çırağan Palace Kempinski Hotel across the main road (see page 103).

ⓐ Yıldız Parkı, Çırağan Caddesi ⓣ 0212 261 8460 ⓛ 09.00–18.00 (summer); 09.00–17.00 (winter); free admission ⓝ Bus: 40T, DT1 or DT2 from Taksim Square

▲ From the workshop of Evi Han

CULTURE

Askeri Müzesi (Military Museum)

The Military Museum can be reached on foot from Taksim Square
in less than 20 minutes, or you can hop on any of the buses
trundling up Cumhuriyet Caddesi from the square. The best reason
for coming here is not so much to gawk at the cannons, weaponry
and uniforms of the Ottoman period – the embroidered tents are
well worth seeing – but to catch the marching band which plays
outside from 15.00 every day that the museum is open. The rousing
music comes from the Mehter Band, dating back to 1289 when
it was composed of janissaries who accompanied the sultan
into battle.

ⓐ Vali Konaği Caddesi, Harbiye ⓣ 0212 233 2720 ⓛ 09.00–17.00
Wed–Sun, closed Mon & Tues

Dolmabahçe Palace

Situated on the Bosphorus waterfront, this was the residence of
the Ottoman sultans after it was built in the mid-19th century.
A baroque pile of a place, its sheer theatricality and unashamed
luxury was an attempt by the Ottomans to reassert imperial
glamour at a time when the empire was in decline. There are two
sections, each covered by its own guided tour. If you are short of
time, take the Selamlık one because this takes in the magnificent
Ceremonial Hall, where you will jaw-drop at the sight of the
chandelier (reputedly the heaviest in the world) and the gilt
dripping off everything around you.

ⓐ Dolmabahçe Caddesi, Beşiktaş ⓣ 0212 236 9000
ⓛ 09.00–16.00 Tues, Wed & Fri–Sun, closed Mon & Thur;
admission charge

Şâle Köşkü (Sale Pavilion)

The Sale Pavilion is at the top of the hill in Yıldız Parkı, but there is a road up to it and you can take a taxi if the climb does not appeal. The first section of the pavilion was modelled on a Swiss chalet, while the other two were specially designed to receive state visits from Kaiser Wilhelm II at the end of the 19th century. The guided tour is mandatory and points out that the large Hereke carpet you see was hand-knotted by 60 weavers and that part of a wall had to be knocked down to accommodate it. More eye-catching is the overall effect of the design that mixes Islamic with baroque and rococo styles. You can decide for yourself if it works or not.

ⓐ Yıldız Parkı, Çırağan Caddesi ⓣ 0212 259 4570 ⓛ 09.00–17.00 Tues, Wed & Fri–Sun, closed Mon & Thur (summer); 09.00–16.00 Tues, (winter); admission charge

RETAIL THERAPY

See page 44 ('Something for nothing') for walking directions that take in the Çukurcuma shops below.

AvantGardeEast Near Galatasaray, this is one of the more diverting clothes shop on the main drag of İstiklal Caddesi. No designer-name outfits, but a creative selection of funky gear for anti-fashion dressing up. ⓐ İstiklal Caddesi 230 ⓣ 0212 245 1507 ⓛ 09.00–21.30

Biz Wear Sells the designs of two sisters. Come here for some unusual fabrics and matching accessories. ⓐ Hayriye Caddesi 20 ⓣ 0212 244 5676 ⓛ 10.00–19.00 Tues–Sat, 11.00–19.00 Sun, closed Mon

Evi Han Kristin Evihan's workshop for making glass beads is in the shop – it resembles Francis Bacon's studio – and this delightful Aladdin's cave retails unique jewellery, accessories, dresses and skirts that you will not find anywhere else. Men have to make do with a choice of cuff-links. ⓐ Altıpatlar Sokak 8, Çukurcuma ⓕ 0212 244 0034 ⓦ www.evihan.com ⓛ 10.00–19.00 Tues–Sat, 11.00–19.00 Sun, closed Mon

Leyla Not a single item of clothing in this shop is from the 20th century, never mind the present one, and you can look here for that special bed cover, pillow cover, jacket, scarf or hat. Quite an amazing little emporium. ⓐ Altıpatlar Sokak 10, Çukurcuma ⓕ 0212 293 7410 ⓛ 10.00–18.00 Mon–Sat, closed Sun

Le Cave If you have come to realise that Turkey is producing some interesting wines, then this discriminating and knowledgeable wine store is worthy of a reconnaissance trip for that special bottle or two to bring home. ⓐ Sıraselviler Caddesi 207, Taksim ⓕ 0212 243 2405 ⓦ www.lacavesarap.com

Mavi Jeans The jeans of choice for jet-setting Istanbullas below the age of 30. ⓐ İstiklal Caddesi 212 ⓕ 0212 249 3758 ⓛ 10.00–22.00

Mephisto Five levels of Turkish music, with everything from traditional folksy to New Age Sufi, plus the usual international big names. A café is on the premises. ⓐ İstiklal Caddesi 197 ⓕ 0212 249 0687 ⓛ 09.00–24.00 Mon–Thur, 09.00–01.00 Fri & Sat, 10.00–23.00 Sun

◀ *Tradition meets beauty at Dolmabahçe Palace*

Ottoman Silk kaftans and bead necklaces from Syria, Afghanistan and Anatolia in this most exotic of Çukurcuma's many intriguing shops. ⓐ Kuloğlu Mah, Altıpatlar Sokak 28 ⓣ 0212 245 8128 ⓒ 10.00–18.00

Tombak II This little emporium of the old and ancient is facing you when you walk to the bottom of the street that Evi Han and Leyla are on. It is stuffed with small antiques, jewellery, tin boxes from yesteryear, memorabilia, collectibles, and old suitcases, big and small, which could have come off the Orient Express. ⓐ Faik Paşa Yokusu 34, Çukurcuma ⓣ 0212 244 3681 ⓒ 10.00–18.30

TAKING A BREAK

Hacı Abdullah £ ❶ Although this venerable establishment makes a strong claim to being the oldest, still-functioning restaurant in the city, the feel of the place is remarkably contemporary. No alcohol, and Ottoman dishes all the way. It's worth a visit just to see the stained-glass dome above the mezzanine floor. ⓐ Sakızağaci Caddesi 17, off İstiklal Caddesi ⓣ 0212 293 8561 ⓒ 11.00–22.30

Hacı Baba £ ❷ An old favourite with shoppers, almost as old as Hacı Abdullah but serving alcohol. The food is tasty and affordable and there is a terrace for outdoor meals in the shade. ⓐ İstiklal Caddesi 49 ⓣ 0212 244 1886 ⓒ 12.00–24.00

Mado £ ❸ Two levels for ice cream, cakes and coffees at Ortaköy's smartest joint; grab a table by the window for views outside. ⓐ Iskele Square, Ortaköy ⓣ 0212 227 3876 ⓒ 07.30–02.00

Nature & Peace £ ❹ One of the first restaurants in Istanbul to feature vegetarian meals and still one of the very few places where you can enjoy tofu- and *sitan*-based dishes. ⓐ Büyükparmakkapi Sokak 21-3, off İstiklal Caddesi ❶ 0212 252 8609 ❷ 11.30–24.00

AFTER DARK

Restaurants

Anjelique ££–£££ ❺ The bar and the martini menu are a big draw, plus the relaxed mood of the place and the scene looking out across the water. There is an evening menu of gourmet pizzas and excellent seafood. ⓐ Salhane Sokak 10, off Muallim Naci Caddesi, Ortaköy ❶ 0212 327 2844 ❷ 12.00–02.00

Changa £££ ❻ Get in the mood with a special cocktail, *satsuma caipiroska* (vodka, tangerine and bergamot), and get down to the fusion-but-not-confusion menu. New Zealander Peter Gordon was and remains the consultant chef so expect some surprises. A tasting menu for two is 100 YTL. The décor is a mix of Modernist art and the proto-industrial and, one claim to fame, a glass window set into the floor above the kitchen. The owners and Peter Gordon have their own restaurant, The Providores, in London's Marylebone High Street. ⓐ Sıraselviler Caddesi 87, Taksim ❶ 0212 249 1348 ❷ 18.00–01.00 Mon–Sat, closed Sun

Miyako £££ ❼ OK, it is a hotel restaurant but this is the *numero uno* place for satisfying those Japanese taste buds that other cuisines cannot reach. The set dinners include sushi, sashimi, tempura and teriyaki while the à la carte choices feature a sublime hot appetiser – seafood in motoyaki sauce – and some spicy

seafood. ⓐ Swissôtel The Bosphorus ⓣ 0212 326 1100 ⓛ 19.00–23.00
Tues–Sun, closed Mon

Reina £££ ⓞ The setting is everything – by the water under the
Bosphorus Bridge – and diners come here to be seen as much as to
enjoy the food. ⓐ Muallim Naci Caddesi 10, Ortaköy ⓣ 0212 259 5919
ⓦ www. reina.com.tr ⓛ 18.30–23.30

⬤ *Taksim by day*

Tügra £££ ➒ Perhaps the ultimate in Bosphorus views, the setting for an evening at the Tügra is indeed magnificent and the terrace setting beckons in summer. The food is Ottoman and there is live traditional Turkish music. A place to spoil yourself. ➌ Çırağan Palace Kempinski Hotel, Çırağan Caddesi 84 ➊ 0212 326 4646 Ⓦ www.cirigan-palace.com ⌚ 19.00–23.00

Vogue £££ ➓ The Mediterranean and Californian fusion dishes, and an astonishing choice of sushi, are as excellent as the views of the Bosphorus. Alfresco in the summer; chrome-and-white design all year. ➌ Spor Caddesi, BJK Plaza A Blok 13 ➊ 0212 227 2545/4404 ⌚ 11.30–02.00

Clubs & cinemas
AFM Fitaş Nearly a dozen screens for Turkish and English-language movies showing all the current releases. This multiplex is at the top end of İstiklal Caddesi, almost at Taksim Square, and there is an English-style pub and restaurant in the same building. ➌ İstiklal Caddesi 24 ➊ 0212 251 2020

THE ORTAKÖY SCENE
Through the long summer nights, the waterside scene at Ortaköy pulsates with social life in the bars and restaurants that crowd the quayside and the cobbled byways that lead to more clubs and pubs in tiny ex-fishermen's cottages. Where you end up is likely to be decided by where you can find a table, so just wander about and see what comes up. Sipping a Mojito while waiting for the sun to go down could make for a scene to remember.

Blackk Located on the same waterfront street as Mado (see page 110), Blackk is an expensive and oh-so trendy restaurant until 23.00 and then it transforms into a nightclub. The elegant tables become bar stands and the black décor gets blacker when the lights dim. 🅐 Muallim Naci Caddesi 119, Ortaköy 🅣 0212 236 7256 🅛 20.00–04.00 Tues–Sat, closed Sun & Mon

Emek Cinema The street housing this historic cinema runs off İstiklal Caddesi. It is a real treat, a rococo-style picture palace with 875 seats and majestic décor, chosen (with good reason) to host the Istanbul Film Festival for the past two decades. 🅐 Yeşilçam Sokak 5, off İstiklal Caddesi

Roxy Expect good gigs at this landmark venue on the Istanbul music scene, attracting a young crowd in their 20s. Famous for serving big bottles of Sex on the Beach and consistently hosting worthy but varied music, from Chumbawamba to Norwegian nu-jazz sensation Bugge Wesseltof. 🅐 Arsian Yatağı Sokak 1, off Sıraselviler Caddesi, Taksim 🅣 0212 249 1283 🅛 21.00–03.00 Wed & Thur, 22.00–04.00 Fri & Sat; admission charge

▶ *Istanbul's attractive skyline*

OUT OF TOWN
trips

Exploring the Bosphorus

A trip along the Bosphorus completes any visit to Istanbul and there
are transport choices to suit your time and inclinations. The most
popular route is the ferry from Eminönü that departs daily at 10.30,
with extra services at midday in the summer, stopping usually at
Beşiktaş, Kanlıca, Yeniköy, Sarıyer, Rumeli Kavaği and, usually the
turn-around stop, Anadolu Kavaği. The trip one way takes nearly two
hours and you cannot hop on and off along the way, so by the time
you have returned you may feel you have seen too much of the
Bosphorus and spent the whole day doing so. When the ferry
reaches Anadolu Kavaği, instead of returning the same way you
could take a bus back to Üsküdar and then catch a ferry from there
back to the European side.

Alternatives include disembarking before Anadolu Kavaği and
returning to Istanbul by bus or taxi or, if you get off at Kanlıca,
catching one of the regular ferries that ply their way back to
Istanbul. The other alternative, taking about three hours in total, is
to take one of the smaller boats that depart from Eminönü and
which usually travel only as far as Rumeli Kavaği, and stop there for
a lunch break before making the return journey. A good-value trip of
this kind is with Turyol – you will see their boats at Eminönü – who
go as far as the second Bosphorus bridge, the Faith Sultan Mehmet
Bridge. Trips like these depart only when full but that does not
usually take too long in the summer.

A boat trip on the Bosphorus is not compulsory and you may
wish to explore the area on land. Buses are frequent from Eminönü
and Taksim Square and taxi rides are not inordinately expensive.
The last bus back from Rumeli Kavaği to Eminönü is usually around
22.00, but if you wish to linger longer, you can catch a bus from

Rumeli Kavaği for the short hop to Sariyer, and from there later buses run back to Taksim and Eminönü.

Cruise tours on the Bosphorus are run by the following:

International Travel Services offer morning and afternoon cruises. ❶ 0212 275 1870 Ⓦ www.dailycitytours.com

Istanbul City Tours provide yacht tours and night dinner cruises. ❶ 0212 237 9898 Ⓦ www.istanbulcitytours.com

Senkron Travel Agency have half-day afternoon cruises. ❸ Arasta Bazaar 51, Sultanahmet ❶ 0212 638 8340

SIGHTS & ATTRACTIONS

Arnavutköy

Arnavutköy, on the European side and halfway between the Bosphorus and the Faith bridges, retains more of its waterside village charms than most locations this close to the shore. The grand wooden houses, *yalıs*, by the waterfront are attractive, and away from the shoreline there are more picturesque homes built from wood.

Ⓝ Bus: B2 & 40A from Taksim, 25A from Eminönü

Bebek & Hıdıv Sarayı

Bebek, where some of the seriously rich have their second homes, is a 15-minute stroll from Arnavutköy along a promenade and, amid all the restaurants, shoreline cafés and speciality shops, is Hıdıv Sarayı (Khedive's Palace), now the Egyptian Consulate. A lovely art nouveau building built by the last khedive of Egypt, it is situated by the ferry stop. Cevdet Paşa Caddesi is the

❶ *The Maiden's Tower, on the Bosphorus*

Bosphorus-facing main street and there is an attractive park suitable for picnicking.

Bosphorus Bridge

This was the first bridge to be built across the Bosphorus, if you don't include the pontoon bridges erected by the Persians when they attempted to conquer the ancient Greeks. It was finished on 29 August 1973 to mark the 50th anniversary of the inauguration of the Turkish Republic. A graceful structure and ranked as the sixth longest in the suspension bridge world league, it measures 1,560 m (5,120 ft) in length. If you were 64 m tall (210 ft), you could touch it when standing on the water below. You can't walk across it; just enjoy the view.

Ⓝ Bus: 40T from Taksim Square to Ortaköy

Küçüksu Kasrı (Küçüksu Palace)

Küçüksu Palace, on the Asian side, is another building superbly placed for maximum effect when approached from the water. The interior is filled with plush trimmings and accoutrements fit for a sultan, as was the intention when the building was completed in the 1850s. The visual highlight is the grand double staircase that curves up to the entrance.

ⓐ Küçüksu Caddesi, Çengelköy ☏ 0216 332 0237 ⌚ 09.30–17.00 Tues, Wed & Fri–Sun, closed Mon & Thur; admission charge Ⓝ Bus: 15 or 15P from Üsküdar to Çengelköy, 101 from Beşiktaş to Çengelköy

Kuzguncuk

On the Asian shoreline and easy to reach by bus from Üsküdar or a ferry from Beşiktaş, Kuzguncuk is a low-key village with a good restaurant (see page 128) and an interesting Jewish cemetery where

▶ *The magnificent suspension bridge across the Bosphorus*

the tombstones lie flat on the ground. The cemetery dates back to the 15th century, when Jews fleeing the Spanish Inquisition were given asylum in Istanbul. You walk to the cemetery via İcadiye Sokak.
Bus: 15 or 15P from Üsküdar

Rumeli Hisarı (Fortress of Europe)

A fortress built by Mehmet the Conqueror in 1452 in four months, at a narrow point on the Bosphorus, as an opening move in the conquest of Constantinople. Facing it across the straits is Anadolu Hisarı, the Fortress of Asia, and between them a vital supply line to the city was cut off. Used later as a prison, the Rumeli Hisarı is now used in the summer as a venue for the International Istanbul Music Festival. You can walk here along the promenade from Bebek in 15 minutes.

Yahya Kemai Caddesi, Rumeli Hisarı ☎ 0212 263 5305
🕑 09.00–16.30 Thur–Tues, closed Wed; admission charge

Rumeli Kavağı & Anadolu Kavağı

Rumeli Kavağı is the last ferry stop on the European side and a pleasant place to enjoy lunch at one of the many fish restaurants clustered around the jetty. Just as attractive for a meal is Anadolu Kavağı, almost directly opposite on the Asian side, and the place where you are more likely to have lunch if arriving on the main ferry from Eminönü because there is a stop-over here for a couple of hours before the ferry sets off on the return journey. All the restaurants buy their fish locally so it'll be as fresh as it can be. There should also be time, especially if you have brought a picnic lunch, to leg it up to the remains of a Byzantine fortress on the hill overlooking the village.

Step through the door of the Dolmabahçe Palace

CULTURE

Sabancı Müzesi

This art gallery stunned Turkey in 2006 by bringing to the country its most important exhibition ever in the form of 135 works by Picasso, and people travelled here from every corner of the land to see what they never dreamed would be exhibited on home soil. And this is not just a flash in the cultural pan (a Rodin exhibition is planned for the near future), so be sure to check out what is on and consider coming here anyway for the superb gallery restaurant, Müzedechanga (see page 128).

ⓐ Sakip Sabancı Caddesi 22, Emirgan ⓣ 0212 277 2200
ⓦ www.mymerhaba.com ⓛ 10.00–22.00 Tues–Sun, closed Mon; admission charge

Sadberk Hanım Müzesi

This museum incorporates two classically styled *yalis* for its displays of ethnographic and archaeological artefacts. An engaging and eclectic collection that includes Assyrian cuneiform tablets, ancient Greek pottery, a circumcision bed and extraordinarily fine Turkish embroideries.

ⓐ Piyasa Caddesi 27, Büyükdere ⓣ 0212 242 3813 ⓛ 10.30–18.00 Thur–Tues, closed Wed ⓝ Ferry: Sariyer; Bus: 25A from Eminönü

> **Question:** What is a *yali*?
> **Answer:** A wooden summer villa on the shores of the Bosphorus, built between the late 17th and early 20th centuries.

ⓞ *Carry on up the Bosphorus for world-class exhibitions at Sabancı Müzesi*

RETAIL THERAPY

Bebek Badem Ezmecisi A main purchase worth considering in this specialist sweet shop is the almond marzipan, but your sweet tooth may also be seduced by the glass jars of candy that fill the shelves.
ⓐ Cevdet Paşa Caddesi 238, Bebek ① 0212 263 5984

Laleli Zeytinyağları Like Bebek Badem Ezmecisi, this is a family-run shop but this time selling its own olive oils. There is quite a variety and some olive-based bathroom products are also on the shelves.
ⓐ Cevdet Paşa Caddesi 97, Bebek ① 0212 265 6617
ⓦ www.zeytinim.com

TAKING A BREAK

Ali Baba Köftecisi £ Arnavutköy boasts a number of fish restaurants that could be checked out for a night-time visit. During the day, though, it is hard to beat Ali Baba Köftecisi (there are two outlets in the same street) for a lunch of meatballs and *piyaz* (beans cooked in olive oil) followed by one of the simple desserts. ⓐ 1 Cadde 104, Arnavutköy ① 0212 265 3612
🕒 11.00–22.00

Asirlik Kanlica Yoğurdu £ Kanlica, on the Asian side, is famous for its yoghurt and this is not the only place where it can be enjoyed, but it is easy to find and convenient, being situated next to the ferry terminal. ⓐ İskele Square, Kanlica ① 0216 413 9644 🕒 09.00–24.00

Bebek Brasserie & Pastry Shop £ If picnicking in Bebek Park, pick up some pastries here, or tuck into one of their sushi meals. At weekends, between 07.30 and 13.30, their breakfast buffet is a big draw. ⓐ Cevdet Paşa Caddesi 28A ⓣ 0212 257 7270 ⓛ 07.30–23.30

Bebek Kahvesi £ A pleasantly unpretentious café that draws in locals throughout the day and evening for a chat and game of backgammon. Tasty apple pie made daily. ⓐ Cevdet Paşa Caddesi 137, Bebek ⓣ 0212 257 5402 ⓛ 07.30–21.00

Zeynel £ A deservedly famous ice-cream parlour, in the same family since the 1920s, with over a dozen varieties to choose from – including some that, apparently, won't damage your waistline – and some delicious desserts. ⓐ Köybası Caddesi 144, Yeniköy ⓣ 0212 262 8987 ⓛ 09.00–19.00

Lucca £–££ A café that changes its mood as the day progresses, becoming noisy with taped music at night, and during the day is a

⬤ Turkish ceramics are on sale at most market stalls

perfect place for good food and drinks. @ Cevdet Paşa Caddesi 51,
Bebek ① 0212 257 1255 ① 08.00–02.00

AFTER DARK

Restaurants

Sade Kahve £–££ Turkish, bohemian-style café-restaurant on the
waterfront and with the Faith Bridge in view. The café is downstairs but
climb the stairs for the marble-floored restaurant and outdoor tables.
@ Yahya Kemal Caddesi 36, Rumeli Hisarı ① 0212 358 2324 ① 08.30–22.00

İskele ££ A seafood restaurant plonked on a restored and renovated
old pier near the Rumeli Hisarı fortress. @ İskele Meydanı 4/1, Rumeli
Hisarı ① 0212 263 2997 ① 18.30–23.00

İsmet Baba ££ A great, waterfront fish restaurant where visitors
from abroad are few in number but the *mezes* (Turkish starters) are
a feast and the fish always fresh. @ Acadiye Caddesi 96, Kuzguncuk
① 0216 333 1232 ① 11.30–23.00

Lacivert ££–£££ This place is under the Faith Sultan Mehmet Bridge
and the restaurant boat will pick up diners from the European side.
Mediterranean cuisine with a Turkish accent, and an above-average
wine list. @ Körfez Caddesi 57, Anadolu Hisarı ① 0216 413 4224
Ⓦ www.lacivertrestaurant.com ① 11.00–23.00

Müzedechanga ££–£££ Views of the Bosphorus wherever you sit in
this glass-fronted restaurant at the Sabancı Müzesi and crafted
Turkish delights like *karanfilli köfte* (carnation Turkish meatballs),
zeytinyağ kereviz (olive-oil-based celery roots) and *pişmaniye*

(Turkish-style cotton candy). ❸ Sakip Sabancı Caddesi 22, Emirgan ❶ 0212 323 0901 ❿ www.changa-istanbul.com ❶ 10.30–22.00 Wed–Sat, 10.30–17.00 Sun & Tues, closed Mon

Körfez £££ One of the most posh places to eat on the Asian side, this fish restaurant has a well-established reputation for quality service and good food. ❸ Körfez Caddesi 78, Kanlıca ❶ 0216 413 4314 ❶ 11.00–16.00 & 18.30–23.00

Poseidon £££ As the name and location would suggest, this is a seafood restaurant and the most glamorous place for dining and wining in Bebek. ❸ Cevdet Paşa Caddesi 58, Bebek ❶ 0212 263 3823 ❶ 12.00–01.00

ACCOMMODATION

Bebek £££ A plush and expensive hotel where the best rooms have their own balconies overlooking the Bosphorus (viewless rooms benefit from a hefty discount). ❸ Cevdet Paşa Caddesi 34, Bebek ❶ 0212 358 2000 ❿ www.bebekhotel.com.tr

Bosphorus Paşa £££ A Special-status hotel on the Asian side, a tastefully renovated *yali* (wooden summer villa) with large rooms and a rather posh restaurant. ❸ Yalıboyu Caddesi 64, Beylerbeyi ❶ 0216 422 0012 ❿ www.relaischateaux.fr/bosphorus

Sumahan on the Water £££ On the Asian shoreline, with private waterfront, six rooms and 12 suites and a private launch service across the Bosphorus. ❸ Çengelköy ❶ 0216 422 8000 ❶ 0216 422 8008 ❿ www.sumahan.com

Into Asia

It is easy to hop across the Bosphorus from one of the many daily ferries that depart from Eminönü or Karaköy and, if Üsküdar is your destination instead of Karaköy, there are also ferries from Beşiktaş. A suggested itinerary for a full day's excursion is to catch a morning ferry to Kadıköy and walk up to Bahariye Caddesi to explore the shops, cafés and restaurants. After lunch, walk back to Rıhtım Caddesi, the road facing the sea, and take a *dolmuş* (mini-van) for a ten-minute journey to Üsküdar. The *dolmuş* stop for the mini-vans to Üsküdar is clearly marked on Rıhtım Caddesi. After exploring Üsküdar, take a ferry back from there to the European side. Ferrying out to the Princes' Islands can be a full-day excursion in itself.

> ❶ When travelling on the ferry to Kadıköy, do not disembark at the first stop – this is Haydarpaşa Railway Station – but the second and main stop at the Kadıköy terminal.

SIGHTS & ATTRACTIONS

Kadıköy
Bahariye Caddesi

This is the street in Kadıköy to head for after disembarking from the ferry. Turn to the right after exiting the terminal and walk along to the main junction, where Chicken Last Stop (see 'Taking a break' page 136) stands, and cross the road to take the main street uphill, Söğütüçeşme Caddesi, that begins next to the big, blue-glassed

❶ *A view across the Bosphorus into Asra*

Türkiye Bankasi. Continue up this street until you reach the junction with the sculptured metal bull in the middle and turn to the right for Bahariye Caddesi. Filled with shops and places to eat, the side-streets running off on either side are the ones to explore for funky little cafés, bars and restaurants.

Princes' Islands

Nine islands in the Sea of Marmara make up the Princes' Islands and the ferries from Istanbul stop by at the four largest. The ferries, nearly ten a day in summer, depart from a dock at Sirkeci, by the

○ *Observing the properties at the Yeni Valide Camıı in Üsküdar*

railway station, and an early departure (09.00 is the first departure) on a weekday is advisable to avoid the crowds. The ferry stops at Kadıköy on the way and then out to sea for Kınalıada, the first of the four islands, then Burgaz Adasi, Heybeliada and finally, after about an hour and a half from Sirkeci, Büyükada.

Heybeliada is perhaps the most pretty of the four and is well provided for in terms of food and drink. There are a number of delis and bread shops where you could make up a picnic but there are restaurants as well. The beach is small but sandy and there are hotels. Büyükada is the largest island and has more than one sandy beach. Here you will find cafés, restaurants, ATM machines and, if you want to stay a night, hotels.

Üsküdar
Atik Valide Camıı

The hillside location is too far away to reach on foot from the ferry terminal and a taxi is the best way to reach this large and aesthetically very satisfying mosque complex, designed by the hugely talented Sinan (see page 80). Unlike İskele Camıı (see below), the richly decorated interior of the Atik Valide Camıı is worthy of your time. One apse is beautifully covered in İznik tiles, the galleries boast *trompe-l'oeil* paintings and the window shutters are inlaid with mother-of-pearl and ivory. Parts of the complex are presently undergoing restoration, so there may be more to see by the time you visit.

ⓐ Çinili Camıı Sokak, Üsküdar ⓑ 08.00–18.00; free admission

İskele Camıı

Facing you at the ferry port, also known as Mihrimah Sultan Mosque, the more familiar name İskele Camıı translates as Dock Mosque. It was built in the middle of the 16th century for the

daughter of Süleyman the Magnificent and while the inside is disappointingly gloomy, there are good views of the Üsküdar port scene from its colonnaded exterior.

🅐 Hakimiyeti Milliye Caddesi, Üsküdar 🕒 08.00–18.00; free admission

Kız Kulesi (Maiden's Tower)

Offshore from Üsküdar, the tower on the islet is called Maiden's Tower after the legend of an incarcerated princess who died here. It is also called Leander's Tower, pirating the Greek legend of the hero Leander who swam a strait between Europe and Asia (not here but in the Dardanelles hundreds of miles away) to meet his lover Hero in a tower. Film buffs may recall the islet's use as a location in the James Bond movie, *The World is Not Enough*. The tower can't be visited, but it's a sight to be seen clearly from the shoreline or from on board the ferry.

Yeni Valide Camıı

This second of the two mosques close to the ferry terminal is entered through a large gateway and across a courtyard area. It was built in the early 18th century by a sultan in honour of his mother.

🅐 Dempkrasi Meydanı, Hakimiyyeti Milliye Caddesi, Üsküdar
🕒 08.00–18.00; free admission

CULTURE

Üsküdar
Selimiye Barracks

The main reason for arranging a trip to these barracks, used as a military hospital during the Crimean War (1853–6), is to visit the

Florence Nightingale Museum. The part of the barracks where the 'Lady of the Lamp' worked constitutes the museum and visits have to be arranged in advance by faxing a request; the fax should include the photograph page of your passport, the intended time of your visit (giving 24 hours' notice), and the contact telephone number of your hotel (state the room number) so that your visit time can be confirmed.

ⓐ Çeşme-i Kebir Caddesi, Selimiye ☎ 0216 556 8000 or 0216 553 1009 ⓕ 0216 553 1009 ⏱ 08.30–17.00; free admission

RETAIL THERAPY

Kadıköy

Craft Market Suavi Sokak is on your left as you walk up Bahariye Caddesi and you will see the stalls from the corner. Water pipes, costume jewellery, portrait-drawing, and lighters for Fenerbaçhe soccer fans, are just some of what you will find here. ⓐ Ali Suavi Sokak, off Bahariye Caddesi ⏱ 10.00–21.00

Sansettio There are a number of other shoe shops along Bahariye Caddesi, but Sansettio has the classiest selection of boots and shoes for women. ⓐ Bahariye Caddesi 104 ☎ 0216 347 0424 ⏱ 09.00–18.00 Mon–Sat, closed Sun

Üsküdar

Kervan Opposite the ferry, this shop retails cushion covers, gorgeous embroidered quilt covers and a variety of home furnishings, some of which will fit into that extra piece of luggage you bought to carry home your booty. ⓐ Selmanağa Caddesi 89, Üsküdar ☎ 0216 343 9530 ⏱ 09.00–18.30

TAKING A BREAK

Kadıköy

Chicken Last Stop £ On leaving the ferry terminal, turn to the right and this neon-lit eatery is across the road at the first junction you come to. Imported beers (which can be consumed only inside), *börek* (savoury pastries), light meals, cappuccino, latte, mocha and frappaccino are all to be had. ⓐ Yasa Caddesi 1 ① 0216 450 0772 ① 09.00–02.00

Mozaik Café £ Seek out this little café for a pleasant lunch away from the Kadıköy hubbub. Walk up Bahariye Caddesi and turn right into Sakizgülü Sokak where McDonald's stands on the corner. Miralay Nazım Sokak is the first turning on the right and the café is halfway down on the left side. The menu is not in English but you will be able to work it out, consisting as it does of pasta, crêpes, pizza, sandwiches and salads. ⓐ Miralay Nazım Sokak 34, off Sakizgülü Sokak, off Bahariye Caddesi, Kadıköy ① 0216 337 4920 ① 09.00–23.00

Murat £ On the corner of Rıhtım Caddesi where the sign to the My Dora hotel hangs, roughly opposite the ferry terminal, glass-fronted Murat has a huge menu in Turkish but it is best to just see what is on display at the counter and pick what takes your fancy. This restaurant is very popular and fresh dishes are cooked daily. ⓐ Rıhtım Caddesi, Kadıköy ① 0216 338 3737 ① 08.30–23.00

New Antique £ Convenient resting place for a drink and meal after walking up from the ferry terminal and on the same street as a little craft market (see page 135), New Antique has pavement tables under shade and an air-conditioned interior for pizzas and Turkish dishes. ❷ Ali Suavi Sokak 5, off Bahariye Caddesi ❶ 0216 347 3151 🕒 11.30–22.30

Özlem Ipekdal Café £ A funky little place boasting a 'happy hour' of a spaghetti dish with a soft drink for under 4 YTL between 12.00 and 14.00. You will find it when shopping in the craft market off Bahariye Caddesi (see page 135). ❷ Osmanağa Mah, off Ali Suavi Sokak 5, off Bahariye Caddesi ❶ 0216 347 2878 🕒 10.00–20.00

🔻 Architecture befitting a Prince's Island

Üsküdar
Sözbir Royal Residence £££ A hotel (see page 140), across from the ferry terminal, where you can enjoy drinks in the lobby café while gazing out across the Bosphorus or have lunch in the rather posh restaurant that also faces the sea. ⓐ Paşalimanı Caddesi 6, Üsküdar ⓣ 0216 495 7000 ⓛ 07.30–23.00

AFTER DARK

Üsküdar does not have much to recommend it at night and Kadıköy is a far more entertaining area to base yourself if staying overnight or catching a late ferry back. The small streets off Bahariye Caddesi, especially in the vicinity of Mozaik Café (see page 136), are full of little cafés that double up as bars and there are a number of restaurants to choose from. Just give yourself time to get downhill for the last ferry back at 23.00 (check the time when you arrive).

Kadıköy
Restaurants
Garnie £–££ ❼ Easy to find, commanding a prime site by the junction with the metal-sculpted bull where Bahariye Caddesi begins, Garnie is a café-restaurant during the day but at night the fairy lights switch on and live music enlivens the atmosphere. There is a courtyard with tables if the music is too loud. A menu of Turkish dishes, pizza, salads and burgers. ⓐ Nihal Sokak 13, off Bahariye Caddesi, Kadıköy ⓣ 0216 349 8750 ⓛ 09.00–01.00

Cinemas
Süreyya Sineması A 1920s building that opened as an opera house, switching to cinema a decade later and still showing movies. Lots of

original features carefully preserved in the 1990s restoration project. Current Hollywood fodder normally features on the weekly programme. ➌ Bahariye Caddesi 29, Kadıköy ☎ 0216 336 0682 ⓦ www.sureyya.com

ACCOMMODATION

Kadıköy

Hotels in Kadıköy are conveniently situated in the streets running off Rıhtım Caddesi, the main road that faces you as you leave the ferry terminal.

Aden ££ Tucked away down a *sokak* off the main Rıhtım Caddesi, it is almost directly opposite the ferry station. Functional but smart, fine for a one-night stay and with its own restaurant. ➌ Rıhtım Caddesi, Yoğurtçu Şükrü Sokak 2, Kadıköy ☎ 0216 345 1000 ⓦ www.adenotel.com

Bella £££ Next to the Aden but in a higher league, this is a new hotel where comfort and simplicity are modishly aligned. There is no restaurant, though breakfast is included in room rates, but you'll find a *hamam* and sauna downstairs. ➌ Rıhtım Caddesi, Yoğurtçu Şükrü Sokak 2, Kadıköy ☎ 0216 349 7373 ⓕ 0216 449 4372

My Dora £££ Take your pick between My Dora and Bella for they are similarly priced and, although My Dora (signposted on Rıhtım Caddesi) has Modernist touches by way of a polished-steel-and-glass lobby, the bedrooms here are smallish and old-fashioned in their décor, but have modern bathrooms and a mini-bar. There is a

restaurant on the first floor. ⓐ Rıhtım Caddesi, Recaizade Sokak 6, Kadıköy ① 0216 414 8350 ⓕ 0216 414 8353 ⓦ www.hotelmydora.com

Üsküdar

Sözbir Royal Residence £££ Turn to the left after exiting from the ferry terminal to find this hotel on the other side of the road after a three-minute walk. Very plush indeed, the hotel boasts Ottoman-style luxury, with rooms and the outdoor pool facing the Bosphorus. ⓐ Paşalimanı Caddesi 6, Üsküdar ① 0216 495 7000 ⓦ www.sozbirroyalresidence.com

Princes' Islands

Büyükada Princess ££ An attractive stone building and some of its 24 bedrooms overlook the sea, although these cost more. There's an outdoor swimming pool and restaurant too. ⓐ İskele Caddesi, Büyükada ① 0216 382 1628 ⓕ 0216 382 1949

Splendid ££ A hotel that earns its name because of its location on a hill and the simple elegance of the wooden building. It offers an outdoor pool, rooms with balconies and a restaurant. The rooms are not quite as splendid but are fine for a one-night stay. ⓐ Nisan Caddesi, Büyükada ① 0216 382 6950 ⓕ 0216 382 6775 ⓦ www.splendidhotel.net

● *Look out for mobile water-sellers*

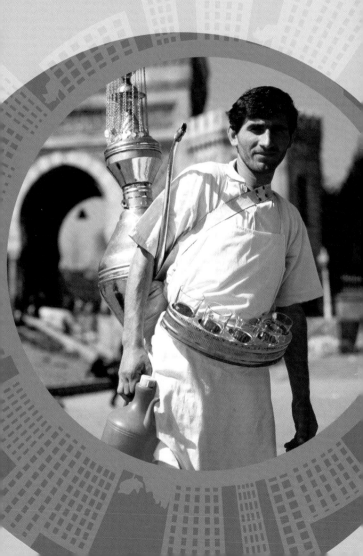

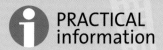

Directory

GETTING THERE

Flying is the fastest option for most visitors but there are also train and road connections.

By air

Turkey's main airline, Turkish Airlines, has three flights a day from London, taking about three and a half hours, and easyJet flies from Luton. British Airways also flies direct, as does Delta Airlines in the US, and Turkish Airlines flies direct from Chicago and New York. Most major European airlines have direct flights from European capitals to Istanbul.

British Airways ☎ 0870 850 9850 (UK) ⓦ www.britishairways.com
Delta Airlines ☎ 1800 221 1212 (US) ⓦ www.delta.com
Turkish Airlines ☎ 020 7766 9300 (UK), 212 339 9650 (US), 0212 663 6363 (Istanbul) ⓦ www.turkishairlines.com

Many people are aware that air travel emits CO_2 which contributes to climate change. You may be interested in the possibility of lessening the environmental impact of your flight through the charity Climate Care, which offsets your CO_2 by funding environmental projects around the world. Visit www.climatecare.org

By rail

No, it is not possible to take the Orient Express to Istanbul but, if you have a lot of time and love trains, you can spend three nights and four days getting there from London via Brussels, Vienna and

◗ The Fountain of Life *(1904) by Osman Bey*

Budapest. It will take less time from cities in the European continent but the cost is still likely to exceed an air fare. European travellers will save some money with an Inter-Rail pass.

Rail Europe Ⓦ www.raileurope.co.uk (UK),
www.eurorailways.com (US)

The Man in Seat 61 Ⓦ www.seat61.com

Thomas Cook European Rail Timetable ☎ 01733 416477 (UK), 1800 322 3834 (US) Ⓦ www.thomascookpublishing.com

By road

Unless you want to drive through Hungary, Romania and Bulgaria, the more familiar road route is through France, Italy and Greece, with the option of a direct ferry from Italy to the west coast of Turkey and then a drive to Istanbul. Registration documents and driving licences need to be brought with you. Check with your insurance company regarding insurance cover.

Package deals

A number of companies offer package deals to Istanbul that include flights and accommodation and sometimes they can be good value.

TRAVEL INSURANCE

It is advisable to arrange travel insurance before travelling to Istanbul as there are no reciprocal health schemes with EU countries. A good policy will cover medical treatment, baggage cover and theft or loss of possessions. You will need to make a police report for non-medical claims and ensure you keep any receipts for medical treatment. Consider keeping a copy of your policy and emergency contact numbers in your email account.

Links to such companies and deals can be found on
www.gototurkey.co.uk, and include the following:

Adelphi Tours ⓦ www.adelphitours.com

Anatolian Sky Holidays ☎ 0870 504040 (UK) ⓦ www.anatolian-sky.co.uk

Cachet Travel ☎ 020 8847 8700 (UK) ⓦ www.cachet-travel.co.uk

ENTRY FORMALITIES

Documents

As well as a current passport with at least three months' validity
remaining, you may require a visa (see www.tourismturkey.org).
These are issued at Istanbul's Atatürk International Airport, or your
point of entry into the country, and are not available in advance
from a Turkish embassy or consulate. For citizens of the UK, the cost
is £10; for Ireland, €15; for the US, $26. The three-month visa needs to
be purchased in cash, so have the exact amount with you in your
home currency when you arrive. Citizens of Denmark, France,
Germany, Greece, New Zealand (and some other non-EU countries)
do not require a visa. Costs vary for other nationalities.

Customs

Import limits for EU and non-EU travellers include two litres of
spirits or wine and 1,000 cigarettes. There are strict rules on the
export of antiquities, including antique carpets, and any reputable
antique dealer should be able to advise you on this and arrange for
the necessary paperwork.

MONEY

The new Turkish lira (YTL) has replaced the old Turkish lira (TL),
making the old notes obsolete. YTL notes are in denominations of

1, 5, 10, 20, 50 and 100. One new lira, equal to a million old lira, is divided into 100 new kurus (YKr). YTL coins are in denominations of 1, 5, 10, 25 and 50 kurus and there is also a 1 lira coin.

Currency can be exchanged in banks and exchange offices but the easiest way to obtain Turkish money is by using the ATM machines which are found outside banks and are easy to locate. Screen prompts are usually provided in English. There are limits on how much can be withdrawn on any one day and for this reason alone it makes sense to bring some cash in your home currency with you. It helps to have more than one bank debit card and/or, as a backup, some Thomas Cook or American Express traveller's cheques in US dollars, sterling or euros.

Credit cards are readily accepted in many hotels, shops and restaurants but, especially in shops and restaurants, you will avoid the risk of being charged a commission by paying in cash.

MONEY NOTES

❶ You should not accept the old Turkish lira notes, easy to spot as they are all numbered in millions – 1,000,000, 5,000,000, 10,000,000, and so on.

❶ Check higher-denomination YTL notes to make sure a 1 YTL note has not been altered to look like a 50 YTL or 100 YTL note.

HEALTH, SAFETY & CRIME

There are no compulsory vaccinations but your doctor may advise inoculation against hepatitis A and B, tetanus and typhoid.

Tap water is chlorinated and safe for brushing teeth but for drinking it is best to use the bottled water that is available everywhere in the city. Should you suffer from a mild stomach complaint or diarrhoea, pharmacies (*eczane*) sell standard treatments and oral rehydration salts. Pharmacies have English-speaking staff and should be consulted for minor complaints. Should you require more attention and prescription drugs, there are many excellent public and private clinics (*poliklinik*) in Istanbul. Private hospitals are preferable to state hospitals. See the 'Emergencies' section (page 156) for contact details.

Istanbul is as safe as any other major European city and common sense dictates precautions as regards personal possessions and safety. Pickpockets operate in crowded places like the bazaars and Istiklal Caddesi. You will see a lot of police around; those on motorbikes, so-called dolphin police, are a rapid-response force while the ones with white caps are traffic police, and either can be approached in an emergency.

Have a list of your traveller's cheques numbers and keep this with your proof of purchase (which will be needed for a claim) and the contact number to use in case the cheques are lost or stolen. Keep this information separate from the cheques themselves;

HEALTH INFORMATION

American travel advice ⓦ www.cdc.gov/travel and www.healthfinder.com
British government health and travel advice
ⓦ www.doh.gov.uk/travellers and www.fco.gov.uk/travel
Travel Health UK online ⓦ www.travelhealth.co.uk
Travel information on various countries
ⓦ www.brookes.ac.uk/worldwise
Useful tips and information ⓦ www.tripprep.com
World Health Organization ⓦ www.who.int/en

posting them to an email account is a good idea. Keep a photocopy of the main page of your passport and the page with the stamp of your Turkish visa and keep these separate from your passport. Consider keeping the number of your passport, or a scanned copy of the relevant pages, in an email which can be retrieved if necessary.

See page 156 for emergency contact telephone numbers.

OPENING HOURS

Opening hours of museums and attractions are usually from 08.30 or 09.00 to 17.30 or 18.00 and some smaller places close for a lunch hour. Government office hours are 08.00 to noon and 13.30 to 17.00, Mon–Sat. Banks have similar hours but open at 08.30. General shopping hours are 09.00 to 17.00, Mon–Sat, but many stay open until 19.00 or 20.00. Markets are open from around 08.30 to around 18.30.

TOILETS

Public toilets are easy to find in Istanbul, marked *Bay* for men and *Bayan* for women, but are mostly of the squat type and are not always kept clean. An attendant is usually around to collect a small charge and may supply toilet paper but don't rely on this; carry your own anyway. Many travellers prefer to make use of hotels' flush toilets and the facilities in any good restaurant they visit.

CHILDREN

There are not that many sites or attractions that are obviously suited to children and hours spent in mosques and museums are likely to bore them. One exception is the Archaeological Museum (see page 63), which has a special children's section, including hands-on models of the Trojan Horse and a medieval castle for clambering about in. The underground Basilica Cistern (see page 62) is also capable of engaging children's interest.

On the plus side, children are adored by Turkish people and there will be few problems accommodating them in restaurants and hotels. Children under six usually stay for free in hotels, with a 50 per cent discount for those aged between 12 and 15. Some of the better hotels will provide cots and arrange baby-sitting through an agency. Baby foods and disposable nappies are readily available in supermarkets and pharmacies.

By way of excursions, a boat trip up the Bosphorus (see page 116) should appeal to children but in the summer be sure to arrive well before departure time to secure seats with a view. It takes nearly two hours to reach Anadolu Kavağı, the turnabout point on the boat trip, and if this is too long for your children you could always disembark at Kanlıca and then take a taxi across the Faith Bridge to visit Rumeli Hisarı (see page 123). The ramparts and towers of this fortress can be explored by children but there are few safety features so take extra care and don't let them explore unaccompanied. Alternatively, take the 15A bus back from the turnabout point to Kanlıca and then taxi over to Rumeli Hisarı.

Young children should also enjoy a trip to the car-free Princes' Islands (see page 132) where bicycles can be hired and there are donkey rides in the summer.

COMMUNICATIONS
Telephones
Public phones are everywhere and international calls can be made from most of them. All calls are made with telephone cards, though some public phones also accept credit cards. Telephone cards are either of the floppy type (in denominations of 30, 60 and 100 units)

or a more rigid version (in denominations of 50, 100 and 200 units). Both types can be purchased from booths near clusters of telephones or from post offices. Use the 200-unit card for international calls, which are cheaper between 22.00 and 09.00 and all day Sunday. As is usually the case with hotels, telephone rates for calls made from your bedroom have a significant mark-up.

Mobiles

Mobile reception is good and you should be able to make and receive calls and text on your mobile phone. Check with your home network, before departure, as regards the cost of such calls and text messages; they can be exorbitantly high.

Internet

Internet access is readily available throughout the city, either through one of the countless internet cafés or in your hotel.

⬥ *There's no excuse for not having shiny shoes*

Post

The letters PTT (Post, Telephone and Telecommunications) identify post offices, usually open 09.00–1700 Mon–Sat. The city's Central Post Office (ⓐ Şehinşah Pehlevi Caddesi), in Eminönü has a 24-hour section for making calls, sending and receiving faxes and buying stamps. Stamps are available from post offices and PTT kiosks. Post boxes are yellow in colour and labelled PTT and many have slots marked *yurtdışı* (international), *şehiriçi* (local) for Istanbul and *yurtiçi* (domestic) for non-Istanbul, Turkish mail. A standard letter or postcard sent to anywhere in Turkey costs 0.60 YTL, international

TELEPHONING TURKEY

To telephone Turkey from abroad, dial the international access code first (00), then the country code for Turkey (90), then the area code (e.g. 212 for European Istanbul, 216 for Asian Istanbul), followed by the local seven-digit number.

TELEPHONING FROM TURKEY

To make an international call from Turkey, dial 00, the international access code, then the country code, followed by the local area code minus the initial 0, and then the number.

Country codes:

Australia 61	**Canada** 1
New Zealand 64	**Republic of Ireland** 353
South Africa 27	**UK** 44
USA 1	

Directory inquiries: 118
International operator: 115

rates for a standard letter are 0.80 YTL and for a postcard 0.70 YTL. You can find a full listing of prices for parcels and heavier letters on the official PTT website, www.ptt.gov.tr

ELECTRICITY

The electricity rate is the normal European one of 220 V, 50 Hz, which means European appliances will work without a problem. Plugs come in the form of two round prongs so you may need an adaptor. American appliances using 110 V to 120 V will need an adaptor and a transformer. Mid-range and more expensive hotels will have 110-V shaver outlets. See www.kropla.com for more information.

TRAVELLERS WITH DISABILITIES

Istanbul is not fully geared up for travellers with disabilities. Most museums and other places of interest, including mosques, are not well-equipped for visitors in wheelchairs. Streets and pavements can be cracked and uneven and are rarely sloped for wheelchair use. Toilets for the disabled are also uncommon and public transport can present a challenge. Before booking your flight, check with some airlines about the facilities they can offer at Istanbul airport. A guide to international airlines and the facilities and services they provide for passengers with disabilities can be found at www.allgohere.com

CALLING ISTANBUL

For local calls in Istanbul just dial the seven-digit number unless you are making a call to the Asian side from the European side, in which case dial 0216 followed by the number. To call the European side from the Asian side, dial 0212.

FURTHER INFORMATION

Tourist Information Offices

Atatürk International Airport ⓐ international arrivals hall ⓘ 0212 663 0793 ⓛ 24 hrs

Beyazıt Square ⓐ Hürriyet Meydanı ⓘ 0212 522 4902 ⓛ 09.00–17.00 Mon–Sat

Elmadağ ⓐ off Cumhuriyet Caddesi, in front of the Hilton hotel ⓘ 0212 233 0592

Karaköy ⓐ International Maritime Passenger Terminal ⓘ 0212 249 5776 ⓛ 09.00–17.00 Mon–Sat

Sultanahmet ⓐ Divan Yolu Caddesi, northeast end of the Hippodrome ⓘ 0212 518 8754 ⓛ 09.00–17.00 Mon–Sat

Tourist websites

The following two official tourist-board websites provide helpful information and useful links:

www.gototurkey.co.uk

www.tourismturkey.org

BACKGROUND READING

Belshazzar's Daughter by Barbara Nadel. The first of a number of detective stories set in Istanbul by the British crime writer. Others include *A Chemical Prison*, *Arabesk*, *Deep Waters*, *Harem* and *Petrified*.

Constantinople by Edmondo De Amicis. 'A travel book for grown-ups' according to Orhan Pamuk and the 'best book written about Istanbul'.

Istanbul by Orhan Pamuk. Personal memoir and cultural history by Turkey's most famous writer.

For further reading material see www.turkishbooks.com

Useful phrases

Although English is widely spoken in Turkey, these words and phrases may come in handy. See also the phrases for specific situations in other parts of the book.

English	Turkish	Approx. pronunciation
BASICS		
Yes	Evet	Evet
No	Hayır	Hayer
Please	Lütfen	Lewtfen
Thank you	Teşekkür ederim	Teshekkuer ederim
Hello	Merhaba	Merhaba
Goodbye	Nashledanou	Hoshcha kal
Excuse me	Affedersiniz	Af-feh-dehr-see-neez
Sorry	Pardon	Pahr-dohn
That's okay	Prima	Preemmah
To	e/a	e/a
From	den/dan	dan/den
I don't speak Turkish	Türkçe bilmiyorum	Tuerkche bilmiyourum
Do you speak English?	İngilizce biliyor musunuz?	Inghilizh'dje biliyour musunuz?
Good morning	Günaydın	Guenayden
Good afternoon	Merhaba	Merhaba
Good evening	İyi akşamlar	İyi akshamlar
Goodnight	İyi geceler	İyi gedjeler
My name is ...	Adım ...	Adaem ...
DAYS & TIMES		
Monday	Pazartesi	Pazartesi
Tuesday	Salı	Salae
Wednesday	Çarşamba	Charshamba
Thursday	Perşembe	Pershembe
Friday	Cuma	Djuma
Saturday	Cumartesi	Djumartesi
Sunday	Pazar	Pazar
Morning	Sabah	Sabah
Afternoon	Öğleden sonra	Oe'leden sonra
Evening	Akşam	Aksham
Night	Gece	Ghedje
Yesterday	Dün	Duen

English	Turkish	*Approx. pronunciation*
Today	Bugün	*Buguen*
Tomorrow	Yarın	*Yaren*
What time is it?	Saat kaç?	*Saat kach?*
It is …	Saat …	*Saat …*
09.00	Dokuz	*Dokuz*
Midday	Öğle üzeri	*Oegle uezeri*
Midnight	Gece yarısı	*Ghedje yarese*

NUMBERS		
One	Bir	*Beer*
Two	Iki	*Eki*
Three	Üç	*Uech*
Four	Dört	*Doert*
Five	Beş	*Besh*
Six	Altı	*Alte*
Seven	Yedi	*Sekiz*
Eight	Sekiz	*Ohsoom*
Nine	Dokuz	*Dokuz*
Ten	On	*On*
Eleven	On bir	*On beer*
Twelve	On iki	*On eki*
Twenty	Yirmi	*Yirmi*
Fifty	Elli	*Elli*
One hundred	Yüz	*Yuez*

MONEY		
I would like to change these traveller's cheques/this currency	Bu seyahat çeklerini/ bu parayı bozdurmak istiyorum	*Bu sey'ahat cheklerini/ bu paray bozdurmak istiyorum*
Where is the nearest ATM?	En yakın ATM nerede?	*En yaken ATM neredeh?*
Do you accept traveller's cheques/credit cards?	Seyahat çeki/kredi kartı kabul ediyor musunuz?	*Seyahat cheki/kredi karte kabul ediyor musunuz?*

SIGNS & NOTICES		
Airport	Havaalanı	*Hava a'lane*
Railway station	İstasyon	*Istasyon*
Platform	Peron	*Peron*
Smoking/non-smoking	Sigara içilir/ içilmez	*Sigara echilir/ echilmez*
Toilets	Tuvaletler	*Tuvaletler*
Ladies/Gentlemen	Bayanlar/Erkekler	*Baianlar/Erkekler*
Subway	Metro	*Metro*

PRACTICAL INFORMATION

Emergencies

Medical services
For emergency medical attention, use one of the city's excellent private hospitals. The German hospital also has an eye and dental clinic.

American Hospital ⓐ Güzelbahçe Sokak 20, Nişantaşi ⓣ (24 hr) 0212 231 4050 & 0212 311 2000

German Hospital ⓐ Sırselviler Caddesi 119, Taksim ⓣ 0212 293 2150

Emergency phone numbers
Ambulance (for state hospitals) 112
Fire 110
Police 155

Police
Tourist Police Station ⓐ Yerebatan Caddesi 6, Sultanahmet, opposite the Basilica Cistern ⓣ 0212 528 5369 or 0212 527 4503

Lost property
Contact the Tourist Police Station or, for property left on public transport:
Karaköy Gar building ⓐ Rıhtım Caddesi, Karaköy ⓣ 0212 245 0720

Embassies & consulates
Embassies are in the capital, Ankara, but many have consular offices in Istanbul. See www.embassyworld.com for a full list of embassies and consulates.

Australia ⓐ Tepecik Yokuşu 58, Etiler ⓣ 0212 257 7050
Canada ⓐ İstiklal Caddesi 373, Beyoğlu ⓣ 0212 251 9838

France @ İstiklal Caddesi 8, Taksim ☎ 0212 234 8730
Germany @ İnönü Caddesi 16, Taksim ☎ 0212 334 6100
New Zealand @ İnönü Caddesi 92, Taksim ☎ 0212 244 0272
Republic of Ireland @ Acısı Sokak 5, Harbiye ☎ 0212 259 6979
UK @ Meşrutiyet Caddesi 34, Tepebaşı ☎ 0212 293 7540
USA @ Kaplıcalar Mevkii 2, Istinye ☎ 0212 335 9000

EMERGENCY PHRASES

Help! Imdat!/Yardım! *Imdat/Yardaem!*
Fire! Yangın! *Yanghen!*   **Stop!** Dur! *Door!*

Call an ambulance/a doctor/ the police/the fire brigade!
Ambulans/Doktor/Polis/İtfaiyeyi çağırın!
Ambulance/Doctor/Polees/Itfaa-ye chaaren!

INDEX

The publishers would like to thank the following for supplying the copyright photographs for this book: Pictures Colour Library: pages 7, 31, 32, 39, 87, 112, 115, 119, 121, 127, 141, 150; Turkish Culture & Tourism Office: pages 9, 19, 21, 58, 65, 98, 108, 311, 137; Sean Sheehan: all other photographs.

Copy editor: Anne McGregor
Proofreader: Lynn Bresler

Send your thoughts to
books@thomascook.com

- **Found a great bar, club, shop or must-see sight that we don't feature?**

- **Like to tip us off about any information that needs updating?**

- **Want to tell us what you love about this handy little guidebook and more importantly how we can make it even handier?**

Then here's your chance to tell all! Send us ideas, discoveries and recommendations today and then look out for your valuable input in the next edition of this title. As an extra 'thank you' from Thomas Cook Publishing, you'll be automatically entered into our exciting monthly prize draw.

Send an email to the above address (stating the book's title) or write to: CitySpots Project Editor, Thomas Cook Publishing, PO Box 227, The Thomas Cook Business Park, Unit 18, Coningsby Road, Peterborough PE3 8SB, UK.